The Official
National Park Quarters Book

by

David L. Ganz

Includes circulating 25¢ coins that honor America's national parks and the special five-ounce, three-inch diameter silver coins that pay homage to America's coin collectors and investors.

The Official National Park Quarters Book

by

David L. Ganz

ISBN-10: 1-933990-26-0
ISBN-13: 978-1-933990-26-2

Published by:
Zyrus Press, Inc.
P.O. Box 17810
Irvine, CA 92623

Library of Congress Cataloging-in-Publication data.
Ganz, David L. (1951–   )

Cover design by Bryan Stoughton.

The Official National Park Quarters Book by David L. Ganz, includes Index.

Printed in the United States of America

Dedication

To my fellow members of the Citizens Commemorative Coin Advisory Committee:

Philip N. Diehl, first executive director (then director of the U.S. Mint and committee member)
Elvira Clain-Stefanelli*
Reed Hawn
Danny Hoffman
Elsie Sterling Howard
Thomas V. Shockley III
Charles Atherton* (Commission of Fine Arts)

Deceased

Hearing in 1995 before the House Financial Affairs subcommittee on monetary policy, which handled coinage matters. Seated (table, forefront), R to L, Philip Diehl, director of the Mint; David L Ganz, then president of the American Numismatic Association and a member of the Citizens Commemorative Coin Advisory Committee; Harvey G. Stack, Alan Stahl of the American Numismatic Society, Beth Deisher former editor of *Coin World*. Rear of Diehl: Reed Hawn.

I also wish to acknowledge the hardworking staff members of the United States Mint, and the coinage advisory committees it has sponsored, who made circulating commemorative coinage possible with the 50 State Quarters Program and contributed to make the America the Beautiful National Park Quarters Program a reality.

Table of Contents

Table of Contents, Cont.

Preface
By Philip N. Diehl

AMERICA THE BEAUTIFUL QUARTERS in silver are the latest in a series of gold and silver commemorative coins dating back to ancient times. These ancient commemorative coins actually pre-date, by more than 2000 years, the use of coins as a medium of commercial exchange.

As long as 5,000 years ago, Egyptian Pharaohs presented gold tokens as gifts to foreign dignitaries. The use of gold and silver coins in commerce did not develop until 750 BCE, in Lydia, a kingdom located in present day Turkey. The practice was disseminated more broadly when the Persians conquered Lydia in the sixth century BCE. Around the same time, the Chinese began minting gold coins for use in commerce.

For the next 2500 years, gold and silver coins were ubiquitous as a store of value used in commerce. They also were the commemorative coins of their day, honoring battlefield victories, conquering heroes, and the stories that history's winners tell in word, song, and metal.

All this changed in the early 20th century when, in the face of widespread hoarding of gold during the Great Depression, many countries abandoned the gold standard thereby devaluing their currencies relative to gold.

These changes in government policy introduced a new era of gold coinage: today the value of gold (and silver) coins is unrelated to their face value, and they and are rarely used in commerce. Instead, in the case of bullion coins, their value is determined by their weight, purity, and the ever-changing price of precious metals on world markets.

The value of numismatic coins, on the other hand, is determined by a far more complex set of variables. Weight, purity, and current precious metal prices are factors, but often more important is condition, scarcity, age and collector demand for the coin.

The story of the large size America the Beautiful (ATB) Silver Bullion Quarters begins with Congress recognizing there was considerable collector demand for private mint-produced replicas of American coins in large sizes. Eventually, Congress responded to this demand by authorizing the U.S. Mint to produce a three-inch diameter, five-ounce silver bullion version of the ATB quarter.

The result is a series of coins bearing designs honoring National Parks in each of the 50 states. These designs are virtually identical to the designs on circulating versions of the ATB quarters, right down to the denomination.

This fact is worth considering a moment. Today, there are coins with identical obverse and reverse designs bearing the same denomination, yet one is 25 times heavier and struck in silver with a metal content of about $150 and the other is struck in base metal with a value of 25 cents. Only the edge lettering of the ATB Silver Bullion Coin distinguishes its design from that of the circulating ATB quarter. Its edge bears the inscriptions ".999 Fine Silver" and "5.0 ounces."

One can imagine the confusion of a numismatist a thousand years in the future upon discovering coins of such different size, weight and metal content, but bearing the same design, year and denomination. Perhaps, there will be other numismatic evidence, such as this book, to help sort it all out.

THE AMERICA THE BEAUTIFUL QUARTERS are an offspring of the highly successful 50 State Quarters Program that was launched during my tenure as Director of the Mint. As a commemorative series, it is also a cousin of the Modern Commemorative Coin series of the last 30 years.

The Modern Commemorative Series was revived by Congress in 1982 after a previous commemorative series was terminated in the late 1940s in the wake of a history of excesses by Congress. As with all numismatic coins, the balance of supply and demand play a crucial role in determining their value. By the late 1930s, a proliferation of coin programs with excessive mintages mandated by Congress depressed secondary market values of these coins leading to a collapse in collector demand.

Within a few years of launching the Modern Series in 1982, Congress was repeating the excesses of the late 1930s and early 1940s. By the mid-1990s commemorative sales again collapsed, and like 60 years earlier, the program was on a path to termination.

But in 1994, the Mint began a reform campaign that saved the program by persuading Congress to enact strict controls over the number of annual coin programs and their mintages. For the most part, Congress honored these restrictions over the next decade, and the secondary market performance of commemorative coins issued after 1996 improved dramatically.

An advisory committee of private citizens, the Citizens Commemorative Coin Advisory Committee, played a crucial role in these reforms. David Ganz, then-President of the American Numismatic Association, was a key player in convincing Congress that reforms were essential to winning back the confidence of American coin collectors. He also used the CCCAC as a platform to successfully advocate for enactment of the 50 State Quarters Program, the nation's most ambitious circulating commemorative to date.

My years as Director of the U.S. Mint were one of the highlights of my career. During my tenure from 1993 to 2000, we reformed the Mint's troubled commemorative coin program and set the stage for a dramatic increase in secondary market values that endures to this day. We expanded the worldwide market share

The Citizens Commemorative Coin Advisory Committee meets, circa 1994. On left side, L to R, Deputy Director of the Mint Eugene Essner, Commission of Fine Arts Secretary Charles Atherton, David L. Ganz, Danny Hoffman. On right side, R to L, Thomas Shockley, Elside Sterling Howard, Reed Hawn.

of the American Gold Eagle and launched the Platinum Eagle to a resounding market response. We won Congressional approval for the

50 States Quarters Program and marketed it into the most successful numismatic product of all time. And while we were at it, we increased profits paid to American taxpayers five-fold, and earned customer satisfaction ratings equal to Mercedes-Benz.

Today, I again work in the industry as CEO of United States Gold Exchange. I enjoy working with my colleagues in the industry, especially through the newly formed Gold and Silver Political Action Committee (www.goldandsilverpac.com), which protects and promotes the interests of coin investors, collectors and sellers on issues related to federal and state taxation and regulation of precious metal coins.

Finally, with this book as a guide, I hope you'll not only learn how coins intended for circulation have become bullion products, but also how coins intended to be strictly bullion products have turned up having (in some cases) substantial numismatic value.

If you are a collector, I wish you happy investing, for you already know the joy of coin collecting. And if you are an investor, I assure you that you will also be collecting precious metal coins whose value packs a dual potential: the bullion content and the added worth to collectors that gives you a one-two punch. I hope you do well with your precious metal purchase, and also wish you happy collecting!

Philip N. Diehl
CEO, United States Gold Exchange
35th Director of the United States Mint
December 12, 2011

Foreword

By Reed Hawn

ALTHOUGH I'VE KNOWN David Ganz for many years (we may have first met when one of my collections was sold by Stack's at an auction that he covered as a reporter for *Numismatic News Weekly*), we got to know each other very well when we were both appointed during the Clinton Administration to the Citizens Commemorative Coin Advisory Committee by Treasury Secretary Lloyd Bentsen.

The committee met for the first time in Washington in December, 1993, and from then until he left the committee in February, 1996, we met regularly and went through numerous applications and presentations seeking the approval of the committee for a variety of projects that the applicants all thought worthy of a commemorative coin or two (or three if a copper-nickel half dollar was part of the package).

Those meetings were wide open, had spirited discussion, and several constants. By tradition, we always had at least one dinner together (which one of the members hosted) where discussions of the day continued, and politics on a national rather than a local level was always on the table.

The second constant was that at all of those meetings, whether in Washington, at one of the Mints, at a convention meeting of the American Numismatic Association, or elsewhere, David Ganz just kept up a steady stream of argument in the form of a drumbeat to make it a mandate of the Citizens Commemorative Coin Advisory Committee that its jurisdiction included the creation and promotion of circulating commemorative coinage. The law establishing the CCCAC constrained our mandate on circulating coinage, whereas what David effectively did was to nullify that constraint so we were able to exert our influence on a much broader range of coinage.

That was no small feat as we realized at the first meeting that we were not loved as historically the Mint's first outside committee.

My friend, Philip Diehl, who worked for Lloyd Bentsen as majority staff director of the Senate Finance Committee, was initially executive director of the U.S. Mint, and later after his unanimous Senate confirmation, the Director of the Mint, was also a member of the CCCAC. He aptly calls David a virtual "Johnny One Note" on the topic of making sure that we, as a nation, had circulating commemorative coins.

Initially, it was a chorus of one, but gradually all of us on the committee saw the value of having commemorative coinage work for collectors, as well as for the general public. In other words, whatever event, place or person commemorated should be without question, truly worthy of a circulating coin, nationwide, whose issue benefitted the United States as a whole.

We started work on our annual report to Congress in the fall of 1994, with the mint staff preparing the initial draft and our committee members editing it. The mint staff, which had heard David's pitch at every meeting since December, 1993, was tone deaf on issuing circulating commemorative coins, but David sent all of us a counter-proposed draft—originally five or six pages long, later edited to a single paragraph—in which the committee voted unanimously to support circulating commemorative coinage in our report to Congress.

Eventually, this matured to a legislative proposal that became the State Quarters Program—first for all 50 states, then for Washington, D.C., and the five trust territories. I might add that during a break one day at the Mint building in Washington during one of our many working lunches, I told David he'd never get the other members of the committee to go along on the states quarters. He said, yes, he would.

If it weren't for this action by the Committee, we'd have no states quarters, from which it follows that no national parks quarters would have been produced. This in turn subconsciously reminds people that there are still places we must protect, which, in a strange way, helps those of us in the battle we're engaged in to continue almost like a self-fulfilling prophecy.

David has worked with me, anonymously, on a number of other

legislative matters, some of which pertain to the funding of our national parks. The "America the Beautiful" series, which directly benefits the national parks through the collector and bullion investor component of the larger program, is an exciting one—and in the end, as they should, the American people are the beneficiary.

The work that the members of the original Citizens Commemorative Coin Advisory Committee did laid the groundwork for the "America the Beautiful" national park circulating commemorative and collectors' numismatic program. This book documents that program from an author who was truly "present at the creation," my friend David Ganz.

Reed Hawn
Austin, Texas
December 30, 2011

Note of Appreciation
By Arthur L. Friedberg

As THIS BOOK was about to go to press, on December 13, 2011, we learned, in a cost-saving move, Vice President Joseph Biden and Treasury Secretary Timothy Geithner had announced the minting of Presidential $1 coins for circulation would be suspended.

All future coins in the program will be restricted to quantities expected to be demanded by collectors.

So what went wrong?

Simply put, these were coins no one wanted.

Unless the United States follows what has been done in most other countries and eliminates its lowest value bank note (in our case, the $1 bill), an equivalent coin will never be in demand.

Such a fate for these circulating commemorative coins should not have been unexpected to anyone who knows the history of coinage, and, as David Ganz will explain in the pages that follow, this will not be the case for the National Park quarters. Over the next 11 years, at a rate of five coins per year, 56 coins will be issued depicting relevant scenes from each of the 50 states, territories and the District of Columbia.

A coin collector, an attorney, and an elected official in his home state of New Jersey, David Ganz was been able to synthesize the knowledge acquired in these seemingly disparate activities and become an influential voice in the development of the State Quarters Program, and he now calls on that experience once again.

As a collector, he relishes the interest that "circulating commemoratives" bring to the hobby. Without the need to spend more than the face value of 25 cents per coin, a complete collection can be built, showing that coin collecting is not only the hobby of kings, but of commoners, as well.

The number of new collectors from these two programs will sustain the hobby for the next generation.

Interesting from a commercial standpoint is that in addition to the circulating series of quarters the mint is also creating a series of over-sized silver bullion coins with identical designs. These National Park Silver Bullion coins will have a fineness of .999 silver, a diameter of three inches, and weigh five troy ounces each—compared to the copper-nickel version's .705-inch diameter and 1/5-ounce weight.

Nonetheless, they will be legal tender for the same 25 cents each.

Imagine, if you will, an archaeologist centuries from now using these unearthed coins to study our economy and the way we lived. The conclusions are inevitable: In 21st century America, an alloy of copper-nickel was approximately 25 times more valuable by weight than the same amount of silver.

They will also surely claim that as relics of America's cultural patrimony, they cannot be sold, but must be given to museums where they will sit forever, unseen and unstudied, as do tens of thousands of coins in so many of the world's museums today.

On a serious note, these five-ounce coins are the first of their weight and size ever minted by the United States Mint, and their mintage is so far relatively low. Instead of a reeded edge, the edge of these contains inscriptions of weight and fineness, which at first created problems as they tended to crumble the edges of the coin.

This may well be the first time that in addition to having to grade the obverse (heads) and reverse of a coin (tails), it may be necessary, as well, to assign a grade to the edge.

This is a book to help guide the reader through what can sometimes be confusing, but more importantly, convey a sense of this one small part of what many consider the world's greatest hobby.

Arthur L. Friedberg
Coin & Currency Institute
Vermont
December 21, 2011

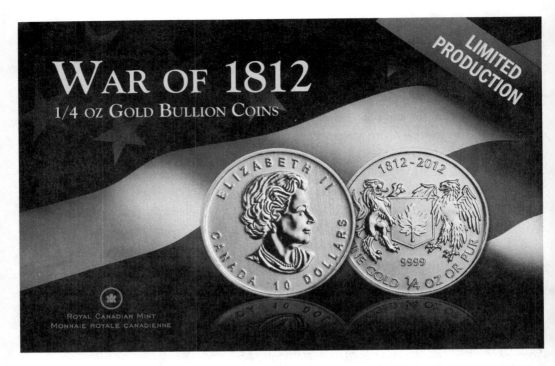

WAR OF 1812
1/4 OZ GOLD BULLION COINS

LIMITED PRODUCTION

ROYAL CANADIAN MINT
MONNAIE ROYALE CANADIENNE

Goldline International is the exclusive dealer for the **Royal Canadian Mint's** ¼ ounce gold bullion coin commemorating the bicentennial of the War of 1812.

The War of 1812 is often described as America's second war of independence. In fact, America's historic national anthem, "The Star Spangled Banner," was penned during Britain's naval bombardment of Baltimore's Fort McHenry.

Available in sheets of 20 uncirculated coins, these .9999 fine bullion coins are qualified to be held in a precious metals IRA.

COIN FEATURES
- 24 karat (.9999 fine) gold content, guaranteed for weight and purity by the **Royal Canadian Mint**
- Uncirculated condition
- Limited production
- Qualified for precious metals IRAs
- Available in sheets of 20 coins.

The obverse (front) of the coin features Queen Elizabeth II in effigy. The reverse displays an eagle, representing American forces, facing a lion, symbolizing forces fighting under British command. Between these two animals is the shield of military conflict which is emblazoned

Goldline
INTERNATIONAL, INC.

To learn more, call 800-661-6599

1601 CLOVERFIELD BOULEVARD, 100 SOUTH TOWER, SANTA MONICA, CALIFORNIA 90404 • www.goldline.com

One Man's View of the Citizens Coinage Advisory Committee

By Donald Scarinci

THE CONTROVERSY ABOUT artistic excellence of American coinage design is the backdrop of the America the Beautiful series. We do not yet fully understand, or appreciate, the effects of the history of this period at the U. S. Mint on the coin designs we see in circulation.

This series of coins is important because it began at ground zero of the attempts by the Citizens Coinage Advisory Committee, working in tandem with the United States Mint, its sculptors, engravers and the members of the "artistic infusion" effort, to fundamentally remake the designs on circulating coinage by improving the art on our coins.

The first time the Citizens Coinage Advisory Committee discussed the America the Beautiful series, we were all concerned about the artistic challenge it presented. How do the artists depict something as grand as a national park on a small quarter-sized pallet; and, given the poor quality of the art we had been seeing up to that point, it begged the question, is the U.S. Mint up to the task?

The small size of a quarter planchet does not allow for sculptural depictions of broad and sweeping vistas. Even though we all knew there would be a large-size version of the quarter that we all began to refer to as "coasters"—the three-inch, five-ounce legal tender, non-circulating coin mandated by Congress—the quarter circulates and that would be the only thing most of the American people every really see.

Graphic designs of parks just won't work on the small quarter. Few sculptors working today have ever been successful portraying landscapes on metal discs.

The CCAC was also concerned about whether the U.S. Mint could produce a series of coins that would distinguish itself as a series and not become intermingled in the mass of pocket change with the previously issued state quarters.

How would the America the Beautiful coins stand out as a series?

From the very beginning, the Commission of Fine Arts and the CCAC expressed their concern that the U.S. Mint create some kind of uniform design element. Without something to unify the coins, the design variations would inevitably confuse the public. It would leave them with nothing to unify the coins as a group in contrast to the state quarters that are now in wide circulation.

At one of the earliest discussions of the America the Beautiful series, John Mercanti attended one of our meetings with a surprise for us. He passed around a pattern design for a rim that his artists had proposed to serve as a unifying element to the series. The rim was elevated and created a recess in the fields where the design element would be placed.

This was the first time since I had been appointed to the CCAC in 2005 that I viewed a mint-created pattern coin. It was an exciting moment and certainly one of the highlights of my tenure on the CCAC.

I held a pattern that was being circulated exactly the way patterns were used throughout the history of numismatics to test and to illustrate how a design or metal would look, feel, and work as a coin. It is very different than seeing a computer-generated design made coin-size.

The fact that a pattern coin had actually been struck and used to show the CCAC and the Commission of Fine Arts what a design would look like was significant. It demonstrated in a real and tangible way that Mint officials were listening to the public, and more importantly, to the committee.

As this series evolves and numismatists study its history, only then will we fully appreciate the extent of the velvet revolution that has occurred at the U.S. Mint during this period, and what impact if any it has had on our nation's coinage.

Donald Scarinci
Lyndhurst, New Jersey
January 3, 2012

Let's Collect National Park State Quarters
The Fun and Profitable Metal Ride

THERE'S A NEW COIN PROGRAM in town designed to appeal to a new generation of coin collectors—the group that started collecting as a result of the 50 State Quarters Program (56 coins when you include Washington, D.C. and the five insular territories). There's every reason to believe it will be as popular or more than the state quarters that brought over collectors by the boatload to join into a fun hobby.

In the last quarter century, coin collecting grew from a sleepy hobby of three to five million people to many more millions of devotees who engage in a frenzied activity. The U.S. Mint says it now has more than 130-million adherents, and they collect for a variety of reasons, not the least of which is the potential for future value appreciation.

People also collect coins to connect with our culture and to gain a deeper appreciation of our history. They like its relationship to economics, politics and the intellectual. It's about investing in history and, incidentally, making an investment that covers other attributes such as value appreciation, some precious metal position and growth potential.

The national park quarters have all this and more. There are three basic components to this series, which is what gives the potential to appeal to an entirely different group of collectors than those who sought out the original state quarters—though some aspects offer the same excitement of being able to acquire coins from pocket change.

First is the standard circulation strike in copper-nickel. That's the portion with the pocket-change appeal. Second is a silver version (the coins are the same size as the copper-nickel issues), designed to appeal to collectors who like proof coins and coins that tell a story, which the national park coins do.

Third is the coinage that duplicates the basic design in a larger-than-life fashion. While five ounce, three-inch diameter coin is legal tender, it really is more of a bullion investment that has a numismatic component. This is something brand new and frankly takes the place of medallic-like issues that private industry sponsored for many years.

With their legal tender guaranteed—if small—it is an entirely different way to collect coins and have a bullion component that allows acquisition in very large, five-ounce increments.

The business of selling legal tender coins of the realm, and medallic, precious metal products has changed dramatically over the last 50 years. Starting in 1964, the Franklin Mint began producing coins of the realm and numismatic and philatelic products and mass-marketing them through a variety of sophisticated mediums.

Like some of the national park quarters, Franklin Mint made oversize silver coins (they didn't do circulation strikes in any real quantity), but that gave a true cache to the silver coins they produced. The U.S. Mint produces circulation strikes, but also proof versions intended for collectors, and (as Congress has mandated), large-sized silver coins similar to copies that have circulated for years in the numismatic community as silver bars or bullion items intended as a means for collectors or investors to acquire silver metal.

Similar to those who acquired the State Quarter Program in the 1999 to 2009 period, most people acquiring national park quarters are doing so out of pocket change (in the first instance), mostly by design rather than mint mark. (In other words, where some albums to house the coins do have slots for uncirculated coins from the Philadelphia Mint and Denver Mint, as well as a proof issue, there are others which only have one coin (mintmark of your choice) for the collection's binder.

This is a different type of collector, and the collection accordingly is different.

Starting in 1982, the U.S. Mint again began to produce non-circulating legal tender coins after a hiatus of more than 25 years (the last issues had been produced in 1954).

Since then, Congress has authorized the minting of more than approximately 240-million commemorative coins, which have resulted in sales of about 54-million pieces, the overwhelming majority of which (4:1 ratio) are proof quality.

This is the trend that the national park series becomes a part of.

As a collector of current U.S. Mint products, the Mint has targeted at least five aspects of what they deliver, and how they deliver it to you:

- Portfolio: At my suggestion, the U.S. Mint eliminated more than 300 unpopular products from its portfolio of 550. This opened up production capacity to make core products, such as annual sets, available for purchase all year round, thus appealing to non-traditional customers like special occasion gift givers.

- Capacity: Additional production capacity allowed the Mint to pioneer new coins, such as the 2009 Ultra High Relief Double Eagle Gold Coin instead of relying on new ways to package and combine existing coins to boost sales.

Old-fashioned 1900 Lafayette commemorative coin.

- Artistic Excellence: A vision for artistic excellence in coin and medal design. The next phase is working with all the design stakeholders to develop a comprehensive artistic excellence roadmap and begin implementation.

- Relief: Believing that the flattening of the obverses of the penny and quarter extended die life at the expense of beauty, the Mint digitally re-mastered them for a more faithful execution of the original designs.

- Quality: The Mint have made major investments in visual inspection systems, digital design, packaging and quality control that have significantly improved the quality of U.S. coins. The Mint now measures coin quality with a comprehensive suite of metrics.

New customers at the Mint—collectors like you who are reading this—are different than the Mint's customers of the past. For one thing, you don't accept production delays, which the older customer simply took for granted.

THE TREASURY AND THE MINT believe that this program is an important one. Here is what then-Mint director Edmund Moy said in the 2010 Annual Report of the Director of the Mint about the America the Beautiful Coin Program:

"Beginning in 2010 through at least 2021, the United States Mint will mint and issue commemorative quarter-dollar coins honoring national parks and other national sites, in accordance with the America's Beautiful National Parks Quarter Dollar Coin Act of 2008 (Public Law 110-456).

"This program honors national parks and sites in the order in which they were first established. Similar to the issuance of coins under the 50 State Quarters Program, quarter-dollar coins featuring five different coin designs will be issued each calendar year of this program.

"In FY 2010, we issued the first four quarters in the America the Beautiful Quarters Program, honoring Hot Springs National Park (Arkansas), Yellowstone National Park (Wyoming), Yosemite National Park (California) and Grand Canyon National Park (Arizona). The U.S. Mint issued 172.9 million America the Beautiful quarters for circulation in FY 2010, which generated $43.5 million in revenue and $21.4 million in seigniorage."

Mint director Ed Moy points out that the America the Beautiful national park coins have something that most other coins don't have— even non-circulating issues:

- To improve current customers' experiences, the Mint cut the amount of time it takes to fill an order in half.
- Raised call center performance standards and redesigned both catalog and public information web pages to make them easier to use.
- Continue to modernize our processes so ordering products and tracking delivery are easy, efficient and seamless.
- Making the Mint consistent with prominent, consumer-oriented retailers.
- As the America the Beautiful quarters debuted in the spring of 2010, the Mint launched a specialized website dedicated to the program: the America the Beautiful Quarters Program website.

- Enhance customer online experiences by providing more extensive information about the individual coins and products and the national parks and historic sites they commemorate.
- The U.S. Mint is also modernizing customer relations by communicating to people in diverse ways.
- The Mint launched Facebook and Twitter sites in July 2010 to broaden customer interaction.
- The Mint is using new media principally to disseminate product and organizational information to current and potential numismatic customers, as well as to obtain direct customer feedback.
- By the close of FY 2010, the Mint recorded 5,010 "likes" on Facebook and had 893 followers on Twitter.

The America the Beautiful National Park Coin Program shows that you can still strike it rich from coins found in your pocket change. That's always been the star attraction of numismatics, and the trend continues today.

Besides those coins pulled from circulation, there is potential for big money in government-issued products produced especially for collectors—many are now composed of different items, in fact, available either from the issuing authority, or the secondary market, which seem destined for substantial future profits.

Mint director Ed Moy with David L. Ganz at Grand Central Terminal, New York City, 2007, on the day presidential dollars were released into circulation.

There are even America the Beautiful coins that you can buy at modest prices that ought to be wanted by every collector, which are genuinely scarce and likely to increase in value in the coming years.

Coin collecting is fun, profitable and lucrative. Each of these lists is no guarantee of future increases in value, but each certainly has the potential to reach for the stars and jump auspiciously in the not-too-distant future.

Chapter One
Price and Product Guide

THE FOLLOWING PAGES HIGHLIGHT the prices received at auction for 2010 and 2011 coins. Teletrade (www.teletrade.com) holds regular mail bid sales (over the Internet) and their prices have been checked for 2010 and 2011. Heritage Auctions (www.ha.com), which conducts Internet and live auctions (and, incidentally, is the third largest auctioneer in the world), has a couple of winners, which are duly noted.

Rejected designs for the reverse of the Mount Hood and Glacier National Park quarters.

What's amazing about the coins in the set is how low the mintages are. Compared to the mintages of Washington quarters in the '70s, '80s and '90s, the America the Beautiful coins are low mintage, averaging 30 to 40 million from circulated versions of the Philadelphia and Denver Mint. In the Washington quarter regular series, you have to go back to 1960 before you can find a low mintage item like this. What all of it says is that these coins are presently scarce, and they're going to be a lot more scarce in the years to come.

YEAR	TYPE	NAT'L PARK	MINTAGE	SALE DATE	GRADE	PRICE (U.S. $)
2011	Unc. Bullion	Chickasaw	25,900	25 Dec 11	PCGS 69	
2011	D	Chickasaw	69,400,000		NGC 68	70
2011	S (proof)	Chickasaw		13 Mar 11	PCGS 70	39
2011	S (silver)	Chickasaw		13 Mar 11	PCGS 70	100
2011	P	Chickasaw	73,800,000		PCGS 67	50
2011	Unc. Bullion	Gettysburg	126,700	03 Jul 11	NGC Unc.	300
2011	S (silver)	Gettysburg		07 Sep 11	PCGS 67	39
2011	D	Gettysburg	31,200,000	07 Sep 11	PCGS 67	
2011	P	Gettysburg	30,400,000	07 Sep 11	PCGS 67	70
2011	S (proof)	Gettysburg		13 Mar 11	PCGS 67	65
2011	P	Glacier	30,800,000	30 May 11	NGC 69	70
2011	Unc. Bullion	Glacier	126,700	03 Jul 11	NGC 69	300
2011	S (proof)	Glacier		01 May 11	PCGS 67	39
2011	S (silver)	Glacier		13 Mar 11	PCGS 70	8
2011	D	Glacier	30,400,000			
2010	S (silver)	Grand Canyon	693,403	07 Feb 11	PCGS 70	120
2010	S (proof)	Grand Canyon	1,222,966	13 Mar 11	PCGS 70	70
2010	Unc. Bullion	Grand Canyon	33,000	20 Mar 11	PCGS 69	625
2010	D	Grand Canyon	35,600,000	31 Oct 11	PCGS 67	55
2010	P	Grand Canyon	35,400,000	01 Dec 10	PCGS 67	39
2010	P	Hot Springs	35,600,000	08 May 11	NGC 67	85
2010	S (proof)	Hot Springs	1,222,966	13 Mar 11	PCGS 70	42
2010	S (silver)	Hot Springs	693,403	02 Jan 11	PCGS 70	110
2010	Unc. Bullion	Hot Springs	33,000	03 Apr 11	PCGS 68	500
2010	D	Hot Springs	34,000,000	04 Oct 11	PCGS 66	8
2010	P	Mount Hood	34,400,000	08 May 11	NGC 69	160
2010	D	Mount Hood	34,400,000	08 May 11	NGC 67	190
2010	S (proof)	Mount Hood	1,222,966	01 Aug 10	PCGS 70	75
2010	Unc. Bullion	Mount Hood	33,000	13 Sep 11	PCGS 68	310
2010	S (silver)	Mount Hood	693,403	13 Sep 07	PCGS 70	140
2011	S (proof)	Olympic		13 Mar 13	PCGS 70	70
2011	S (silver)	Olympic		16 Oct 05	PCGS 70	90
2011	D	Olympic	30,600,000	22 Nov 11	NGC 67	21
2011	Unc. Bullion	Olympic	84,100	27 Oct 11	PCGS 69	22
2011	P	Olympic	30,400,000	08 May 11	NGC 69	600
2011	S (silver)	Vicksburg		21 May 11	PCGS 70	75
2011	P	Vicksburg	30,800,000	30 May 11	NGC 68	70
2011	S (proof)	Vicksburg		13 Mar 11	PCGS 70	85
2011	Unc. Bullion	Vicksburg	33,300	22 Dec 10	PCGS 69	276
2011	D	Vicksburg	33,400,000	22 Nov 11	PCGS 66	63
2010	S (proof)	Yellowstone	1,222,966	16 Jan 11	PCGS 70	120

YEAR	TYPE	NAT'L PARK	MINTAGE	SALE DATE	GRADE	PRICE (U.S. $)
2010	S (silver)	Yellowstone	693,403		PCGS 70	120
2010	P	Yellowstone	33,600,000	18 May 11	NGC 69	130
2010	D	Yellowstone	34,800,000	07 Nov 10	PCGS 67	24
2010	Unc. Bullion	Yellowstone	33,000	01 May 10	NGC 69	2,530
2010	D	Yosemite	35,200,000	20 Feb 11	ANACS 67	6
2010	P	Yosemite	34,800,000	22 Mar 11	ANACS 67	10
2010	S (proof)	Yosemite	1,222,966	13 Mar 11	PCGS 70	25
2010	S (silver)	Yosemite	693,403	02 Dec 11	PCGS 60	65
2010	Unc. Bullion	Yosemite	33,000	01 May 11	NGC 69	719

Key: NGC is Numismatic Guaranty Corp. PCGS is Professional Coin Grading Service. Uncirculated and/or proof coins graded on 1-to-70 Sheldon scale. NGC and PCGS websites used to spot-check prices and no auction appearances. Prices from Heritage and Teletrade.

THE U.S. MINT HAS NUMEROUS WAYS that a collector or investor can acquire the national park quarters, most notably on its website www.usmint.gov.

Still, the Mint has been slow to recognize that their customer base insists on knowing the production figures for each of the products. The Mint drags its heels disclosing this material information, the result of which is that most collectors are forced to buy on the fly.

Perhaps more actively stated, it fosters a lack of trust in collectors and investors.

The chart above shows the mintage (to the extent presently known), a basis for price substantiation (an auction firm generally identified as Heritage or Teletrade, though there are others included), and the service that slabbed it (PCGS, NGC, ANACS, etc.).

Now take a look at the prices, the mintages and the other information. To pull it together in a positive way, here are some of the astonishing conclusions:

- Low mintages on the copper-nickel coins are among the lowest in a half century. You have to go back three generations to the early 1950s to find quarters with mintages so low.
- The five-ounce bullion coins have even lower mintages. Compare and contrast them with the silver eagle (1986 to date) and see how scarce these really are.

- If you want to collect national park quarters in MS-68 condition, or MS-67, you can find many of them already graded by one of the major services for as little as $6-$10 a coin—less than the price of buying it, then encapsulating it yourself.
- Consider the price of many of these coins in MS-70, some with deep, mirror-like finishes, others with beautiful cameos—many are still very moderately priced.
- Some of these coins have no sales records at auction not because they are so rare, but because they are so moderately priced that they are generally sold with their doppelganger: the "P" and the "D" may go together for the copper-nickel or the silver.
- If you collect the large-size quarter dollar design (five ounces, three-inch diameter), the complete collection (assume it is 56 coins) means, assuming one round only, you will have 280 ounces of silver at the end of your quest. At today's prices, this would come to an $8,400 investment.
- This is a series you can collect however you want, and if that method is to do it as a small-sized quarter without regard for mintmark—you are going to have a lot of fun!

Chapter Two
About Our National Parks

IN THE HISTORY OF THE WORLD, the creation of America's national parks was the first time vast tracts of land had been set aside not for the wealthy and politically connected but for the public—"For the Benefit and Enjoyment of the People," as Theodore Roosevelt put it, words that adorn the famous arch at the North Entrance of Yellowstone National Park.

In 1871, the Hayden Survey, which consisted of Ferdinand Hayden's surveyors, scientists, painter Thomas Moran and photographer William H. Jackson, returned to Washington with such an impressive report of Yellowstone's geysers, hot springs and mudpots amidst its beautiful mountains, lakes and rivers that it caught the attention of the American people and, indeed, the U.S. Congress. On March 1, 1872, President Ulysses Grant signed legislation creating Yellowstone as the country's first national park.

Ulysses S. Grant establishes Yellowstone as the country's first national park.

But the story of the early National Park System began a few years earlier when a Scotland-born Calvinist named John Muir settled in Yosemite Valley, California. The amateur naturalist tirelessly roamed the Sierra Nevada mountains, hiking upwards of 25 miles a day with "only a tin cup, a handful of tea [and] a loaf of bread." His journals and subsequent lectures on the value of preserving America's wilderness inspired everyone from presidents to the average citizen.

President Theodore Roosevelt's camping trip with Muir resulted in national park status for Yosemite. In fact, TR would eventually set aside 148 million acres of forest reserves over 50 regional sites.

In 1892, John Muir helped found the Sierra Club, an organization of regular people dedicated to protecting the environment. To many he is known as the "Father of Our National Parks."

John Muir, "Father of Our National Parks," in 1912.

THOUGH IT SEEMS OBVIOUS in retrospect, Congress did not move quickly or unanimously to establish national parks. A look at its rough and tumble history is both informative and tells us why we must be vigilant if the national parks are to remain in the future.

On December 18, 1871, William Horace Clagett, a Republican delegate from the Territory of Montana, introduced H.R. 764, a bill to set aside land on the Yellowstone River for a park: "To set apart a certain tract of land lying near the head-waters of the Yellowstone River as a public park." Samuel Clark Pomeroy, a Republican from Kansas and chairman of the Public Lands Committee, put forth S. 391 (42nd Cong., 2d Sess.) that same day. (Pomeroy, who had served since 1861, was defeated at the next election; whether residents of Kansas opposed the Yellowstone national park is simply open to conjecture).

In January, 1872, Senator Pomeroy, reported the bill out of

committee: "I am instructed by the Committee on Public Lands to report back and recommend passage of the bill (S. 392) to set apart a certain tract of land lying near the headwaters of the Yellowstone river as a public park. It will be remembered that an appropriation was made last year of about $10,000 to explore that country. Professor Hayden and party have been there, and this bill is drawn on the recommendation of that gentleman to consecrate for public uses this country for a public park. Two senators objected, and the report was withdrawn.

Mr. Pomeroy: *The Committee on Public Lands, to whom was referred the bill (S. 392) to set apart a tract of land lying near the headwaters of the Yellowstone as a public park, have directed me to report it back without amendment, to recommend its passage, and to ask that it have the present consideration of the Senate.*

The Vice President: *The Senator from Kansas asks unanimous consent of the Senate for the present consideration of the bill reported by him. It will be reported in full, subject to objection.*

The chief clerk read the bill.

Chief Clerk: *The Committee on Public Lands reported the bill with an amendment in line 19 to strike out the words "after the passage of this act," and in line 20, after the word "upon," to insert the words "or occupying a part of;" so as to make the clause read, "and all persons who shall locate or settle upon or occupy any part of the same, or any part thereof, except as hereinafter provided, shall be considered as trespassers and removed therefrom.*

The Vice President: *Is there objection to the present consideration of this bill?*

Mr. Cameron: *I should like to know from somebody having charge of the bill, in the first place, how many miles square to be set apart, or how many acres, for this purpose, and what is the necessity for the park belonging to the United States.*

Mr. Pomeroy: *This bill originated as the result of the exploration, made by Professor Hayden, under an appropriation of Congress of last year. With a party he explored the headwaters of the Yellowstone and found it to be a great natural curiosity, great geysers, as they are termed, water-spouts, and* *hot springs, and having platted the ground himself, and having given me the dimensions of it, the bill was drawn up, and it was thought best to consecrate and set apart this great place of national resort, as it may be in the future, for the purposes of public enjoyment.*

Mr. Morton: *How many square miles are there in it?*

Mr. Pomeroy: *It is substantially 40 miles square. It is north and south 44 miles, and east and west 40 miles. He was careful to make a survey so as to include all the basin where the Yellowstone has its source.*

Woodrow Wilson creates the National Park Service in 1916.
Library of Congress

Mr. Cameron: *That is several times larger than the District of Columbia.*

Mr. Pomeroy: *Yes, sir. There are no arable lands; no agricultural lands there. It is the highest elevation from which our springs descend, and as it cannot interfere with any settlement for legitimate agricultural purposes, it was thought that it ought to be set apart early for this purpose. We found when we set apart the Yosemite valley that there were one or two persons who had made claims there, and there has been a contest, and it has finally gone to the Supreme Court to decide whether persons who settle on unsurveyed lands before the government takes possession of them by any special act of Congress have rights as against the government. The court has held that settlers on unsurveyed lands have no rights as against the government. The government can make an appropriation of any unsurveyed lands, notwithstanding settlers may be upon them. As this region would only on account of preempting a hot spring or some valuable mineral, it was thought such claims had better be excluded from the bill.*

There are several senators whose attention has been called to this matter, and there are photographs of the valley and the curiosities, which senators can see. The only object of the bill is to take early possession of it by the

United States and set it apart, so that it cannot be included in any claim or occupied by any settlers.

Mr. Trumbull: *Mr. President—*

The Vice President: *The Chair must state that the Senate have not yet given their consent to the present consideration of the bill. The Senator from Pennsylvania desired some explanation in regard to it. Does he reserve the right to object?*

In February, 1872, the House of Representatives debated a Senate bill to create the park. The Journal of the House of Representatives catches the flavor of the debate:

"The bill of the Senate (S. 392) to set apart a certain tract of land lying near the head-waters of the Yellowstone River as a public park, was read a first and second time.

"After the debate, Mr. Scofield moved the previous question, which was seconded and the main question ordered. Under the operation thereof the bill was ordered to be read a third time.

"It was accordingly read the third time.

"The question was then put: 'Shall the bill pass?'

"And it was decided in the affirmative.

"Yeas: 115

"Nays: 65

"Not voting: 60

"The yeas and nays being desired by one-fifth of the members present."

The Senate took note of passage the same day, its debate coming shortly thereafter.

The Globe, page 672, where the bill under debate read as follows:

The tract of land in the Territories of Montana and Wyoming lying near the headwaters of the Yellowstone river, and described as follows, to wit: commencing at the junction of Gardiner's river with the Yellowstone river, and running east to the meridian passage 10 miles to the eastward of the most eastern point of Yellowstone lake; thence south along the meridian to the parallel of latitude passing 10 miles south of the most southern point of Yellowstone lake; thence west along said parallel to the meridian passing 15 miles west of the most western point of Madison lake; thence north along said meridian to the latitude of the junction of the Yellowstone and Gardiner's rivers; thence east to the place of beginning, is hereby reserved and withdrawn from settlement, occupancy, or sale under the laws of the United States, and dedicated and set apart as a public part of pleasuring-ground for the benefit and enjoyment of the people; and all persons who shall locate, ore settle upon or occupy the same, or any part thereof, except as hereinafter provided shall be considered trespassers, and removed there from.

SEC. 2. That said public park shall be under the exclusive control of the Secretary of the Interior, whose duty it shall be, as soon as practicable, to make and publish such rules and regulations as he may deem necessary or proper for the care and management of the same. Such regulations shall provide for the preservation from injury or spoliation of all timber, mineral deposits, natural curiosities, or wonders within said park, and their retention in their natural condition. The Secretary may in his discretion lease for building purposes, for terms not exceeding 10 years, of small parcels of ground, at such places in said park as shall require the erection of buildings for the accommodation of visitors; all of the proceeds of said leases, and all other revenues that may be derived from any source connected with said park, to be expended under his direction in the management of the same, and the construction of roads and bridle-paths therein. He shall provide against the wanton destruction of the fish and game found within said park, and against their capture or destruction for the purpose of merchandise or profit. He shall also cause all persons trespassing upon the same after the passage of this act to be removed therefrom, and generally shall be authorized to take all such measures as shall be necessary or proper to full carry out the objects and purposes of this act.

The Vice President: *These amendments will be regarded as agreed to unless objected to. They are agreed to.*

Mr. Anthony: *I observe that the destruction of game and fish for gain or profit is forbidden. I move to strike out the words "for gain or profit," so that there shall be no destruction of game there for any purpose. We do not want sportsmen going over there with their guns.*

Mr. Pomeroy: *The only object was to prevent the wanton destruction of the fish and game; but we thought parties who encamped there and caught fish for their own use ought not to be restrained from doing so. The bill will allow parties there to shoot game or catch fish for their own subsistence. The provision of the bill is designed to stop the wanton destruction or capture of game or fish for merchandise.*

Mr. Anthony: *I do not know, but that covers it. What I mean is that this park should not be used for sporting. If people are encamped there, and desire to catch fish and kill game for their own sustenance while they remain there, there can be no objection to that; but I do not think it ought to be used as a preserve for sporting.*

Mr. Pomeroy: *I agree with the Senator, but I think the bill as drawn protects the game and fish as well as it can be done.*

Mr. Pomeroy: *Very well; I am satisfied.*

The Vice President: *The Senator does not insist on his amendment?*

Mr. Anthony: *No, sir.*

Lake Yellowstone by Thomas Moran.
Library of Congress

Mr. Tiptoe: *I think if this is to become a public park, a place of great national resort, and we allow the shooting of game or the taking of fish without any restriction at all, the game will soon be utterly destroyed. I think, therefore, there should be a prohibition against their destruction for any purpose, for if the door is once opened I fear there will ultimately be an entire destruction of all the game in that park. Mr. Pomeroy. It will be entirely under the control of the Secretary of the Interior. He is to make the rules that shall govern the destruction and capture of game. I think in that*

respect the Secretary of the Interior, whoever he may be, will be as vigilant as we would be.

The Vice President: *Perhaps the Secretary had better report the sentences referred to by the Senators as being on this question, and then any Senator who desires to amend can move to do so.*

Chief Clerk: *He shall provide against the wanton destruction of the fish and game found within said park, and against their capture or destruction for the purposes of merchandise or profit.*

Mr. Edmunds: *I hope this bill will pass. I have taken some pains to make myself acquainted with the history of this most interesting region. It is so far elevated above that sea that it cannot be used for private occupation at all, but it is probably one of the most wonderful regions in that space of territory which the globe exhibits anywhere, and, therefore, we are doing no harm to the material interests of the people in endeavoring to preserve it. I hope the bill will pass unanimously.*

Mr. Cole: *I have grave doubts about the propriety of passing this bill. The natural curiosities there cannot be interfered with by anything that man can do. The geysers will remain, no matter where the ownership of the land may be, and I do not know why settlers should be excluded from a tract of land 40 miles square, as I understand this to be, in the Rocky mountains or any other place. I cannot see how the natural curiosities can be interfered with if settlers are allowed to approach them. I suppose there is very little timber on this tract of land, certainly no more than is necessary for*

Reverse of the Acadia National Park quarter.

the use and convenience of persons going upon it. I do not see the reason or propriety of setting apart a large tract of land of that kind in the Territories of the United States for a public park. There is abundance of public park ground in the Rocky mountains that will never be occupied. It is all one great park, and never can be anything else; large portions of it at all events. There are some places, perhaps this is one, where persons can and would go and settle and improve and cultivate the grounds, if there be ground fit for cultivation.

Mr. Edmunds: *Has my friend forgotten that this ground is north of latitude 40, and is more than seven thousand feet above the level of the sea? You cannot cultivate that kind of ground.*

Mr. Cole: *The Senator is probably mistaken in that. Ground of a greater height than that has been cultivated and occupied.*

Mr. Edmunds: *In that latitude?*

Mr. Cole: *Yes, sir. But if it cannot be occupied and cultivated, why should we make a public park of it? If it cannot be occupied by man, why protect it from occupation? I see no reason in that. If nature has excluded men from its occupation, why set it apart and exclude persons from it? If there is any sound reason for the passage of the bill, of course I would not oppose it; but really I do not see any myself.*

Stephen Mather, the first NPS Director in 1916.

Mr. Trumbull: *I think our experience with the wonderful natural curiosity, if I may so call it, in the Senator's own state, should admonish us of the propriety of passing such a bill as this. There is the wonderful Yosemite valley, which one or two persons are now claiming by virtue of a preemption. Here is a region of country away up in the Rocky mountains, where there are the most wonderful geysers on the face of the earth; a country that is not likely ever to be inhabited for the purposes of agriculture; but it is possible that some person may go there and plant himself right across the only path that leads to these wonders, and charge every man that passes along between the gorges of these mountains a fee of a dollar or five dollars. He may place an obstruction there, and toll may be gathered from every person who goes to see these wonders of creation.*

Now this tract of land is uninhabited; nobody lives there; it was never trod by civilized man until a short period. Perhaps a year or two ago was the first time that this country was ever explored by anybody. It is now proposed, while it is in this condition, to reserve it from sale and occupation in this way. I think it is a very proper bill to pass, and now is the time to enact it. We did set apart the region of country on which the mammoth trees grow in California, and the Yosemite valley also we have undertaken to reserve, but there is a dispute about it. Now, before there is any dispute as to this wonderful country, I hope we shall except it from the general disposition of the public lands, and reserve it to the government. At some future time, if we desire to do so, we can repeal this law if it is in anybody's way; but now I think it a very appropriate bill to pass.

Grand Canyon National Park

THE DEBATE ON THE FIRST NATIONAL PARK was not long by most standards. Subsequent parks have similarly intriguing stories. Some of the names behind the individual properties are familiar—John Muir, Theodore Roosevelt, John D. Rockefeller—but there were many others, from all walks of life, who worked to preserve some piece of land for the benefit of people they'd never met. It's a testament to their foresight that the national parks have become perhaps our greatest national treasure.

Originally the national parks and monuments came under the auspices of the Department of the Interior, but several prominent conservationists, including millionaire industrialist Stephen Mather, pushed for an independent agency to oversee the protected federal lands. On August 25, 1916 President Woodrow Wilson signed the National Park Service Organic Act.

Today, the National Park Service (NPS) manages 58 national parks and 339 other historical monuments and other conservation and historical properties. The NPS oversees some 84.4 million acres of land, the largest of which is Wrangell-St. Elias National Park and Preserve in Alaska at 13.2 million acres. The smallest property in the system is Thaddeus Kosciuszko National Memorial in Pennsylvania at .02 acres.

The American concept of national parks has spread throughout the world. In the 1970s, the United Nations Educational Social and Cultural Organization (UNESCO) created World Heritage Sites, of which President Richard Nixon was a strong champion. The United States proposed the World Heritage Convention treaty to the international community and was the first nation to ratify it.

The UNESCO World Heritage Convention allows each nation to retain sovereignty and control over its sites, with the understanding all participating nations pledge to identify and protect their key natural and cultural properties.

The Secretary of the Interior, acting through the National Park Service, is responsible for identifying and nominating U.S. sites to the World Heritage List. Proposed sites must be either federal property, such as national parks, or sites already designated as national historical landmarks or national natural landmarks.

Of the 21 U.S. properties on the list of World Heritage Sites, nine are also to be featured in the National Park quarter series: Yellowstone, Grand Canyon, Everglades, Olympic, Great Smoky Mountains, Statue of Liberty (Ellis Island), Yosemite, Chaco Culture and Hawaii Volcanoes.

Chapter Three
Origins of the National Park Quarter

JUST AS THE 50 STATES COIN PROGRAM ended, and a year-long substitute six-coin territorial quarters program was to begin, Congress passed a new coin law. President George W. Bush signed it into law with about a month left in his term of office.

Rep. Michael Castle (R-DE), legislative founder of the Statehood Quarters Program, joined forces with the ranking Democrats on the House Financial Services Committee to sponsor H.R. 6184, as an omnibus measure that would change the way we look at our pocket change—and our national parks—forever.

Introduced June 4, 2008, and passed by the House just about a month later on July 9, 2008, the enabling clause says the purpose is "to provide for a program for circulating quarter-dollar coins that are emblematic of a national park or other national site in each State, the District of Columbia, and each territory of the United States," and for other purposes.

U.S. Rep. Michael Castle with the author at the July, 1995 Congressional hearing from which the State Quarters Program emerged.

The "other purposes" are doozies.

They include a three-inch diameter, five-ounce 90-percent silver bullion duplicate coin that would say "quarter dollar." It is a legal tender, but probably not at any amount higher than its denominated value. It would only be available during the year in which the legal tender coin would be produced.

Struck at the rate of five per year (and, at the option of the Secretary of the Treasury, there could be a second cycle—thus, the program could run more than 20 years), the designs chosen shall be from "the selection of a national park or other national site in each state to be honored."

Choice of the actual design shall rest with "the Secretary of the Treasury, after consultation with the Secretary of the Interior and the governor or other chief executive of each state with respect to which coin is to be issued."

The Mayor of Washington, D.C., the chief executive of the five insular trust territories, and the governors of the 50 states would be consultants. A total of 56 coins at a minimum would be part of the program, over the span of a little more than 11 years (at a statutory rate of five per year).

There is a requirement that the design be chosen "after giving full and thoughtful consideration to national sites that are not under the jurisdiction of the Secretary of the Interior so that the national site chosen for each state shall be the most appropriate in terms of natural or historic significance."

Based on the successful 50 State Quarters Program, Castle stood in front of Independence Hall and the Liberty Bell in Philadelphia on June 4, 2008 and for drama, also in front of the U.S. Capitol in Washington, D.C. on June 9 to introduce a new quarter series honoring national parks and other historic sites.

"I authored the 50 State Commemorative Coin Act more than a decade ago," Castle said. "There has been wonderful feedback from students, educators and coin collectors. Even people who had never stopped to notice their coins before were eager to see what image would be on the next quarter."

Castle defended the legislation by saying "the U.S. Mint estimates that the State Quarters Program will make more than $6.2 billion in revenue, $3.7 billion more than regular quarters alone."

As he described the legislation, Castle said "the bill instructs the U.S. Mint to issue five new quarter designs per year for the 50 states, D.C., and the U.S. Territories. This new program would give us an exciting way to honor our national parks and historic sites, such as Yellowstone or Yosemite National Park or maybe even the Liberty Bell or the U.S. Capitol."

Castle was joined by Rep. Carolyn Maloney (D-NY), an original co-sponsor of the bill and fellow member of the Financial Services

Committee. "The 50 State Quarters Program has been a tremendous success," Maloney said. "This new coin program will give us an exciting new way to continue highlighting the unique diversity of our 50 states by honoring a national park or historic site in each of them and putting it on a coin.

"Heads or tails, this bill is a win for each our national parks, states and our country. It has been an honor to work with my good friend Mr. Castle again on this bill, and I appreciate his leadership."

Rep. Luis Gutierrez (D-IL), also an original co-sponsor of the bill, said, "I am proud to support this legislation, which not only honors our nation's natural and historic treasures, but also benefits the United States Treasury and taxpayer by generating a unique source of revenue."

As Chair of the Subcommittee on Domestic and International Monetary Policy, Trade and Technology, which handled the initiative, Gutierrez added, "I am also pleased that our nation's capital will be appropriately recognized with its own commemorative quarter. It is only

U.S. Rep. Luis Gutierrez (D-IL) co-sponsors National Park Quarters Program legislation.

appropriate, in paying tribute to our history, we recognize the city that has been at the center of law and justice since the days of George Washington himself."

These coins have since been issued in the order the national park or historical site was designated. Sites are not limited to national parks; they may also feature a wildlife refuge or historical place. National parks alone are not employed perhaps because there are no such facilities in Delaware, Castle's home state.

There are also no national parks in Puerto Rico, though there are national historic sites. In deciding which location to place on the coin, the Secretary of the Treasury is required to make the final decision after consulting with the Secretary of the Interior and state governors.

General guidance is offered: "The term 'national site' means any site under the supervision, management or conservancy of the National Park Service, the United States Forest Service, the United States Fish and Wildlife Service, or any similar department or agency of the Federal Government."

It also includes "any national park, national monument, national battlefield, national military park, national historical park, national historic site, national lakeshore, seashore, recreation area, parkway, scenic river, or trail and any site in the National Wildlife Refuge System."

Under the plan, after the first set of 56 coins are produced, the Treasury Secretary can authorize round two for a second dip at America's open space. (As to the possibility of an unexpected 57th coin, see the next chapter).

An amazing second title will allow the Mint to challenge makers of silver bullion medallions that, in the past, have mimicked U.S. coin designs. These would be struck as an addition to the section of Title 31, the U.S. Code section governing money that specifies denominations, specifications and design of coins. Here are the technical specs for the "Silver Bullion Investment Product":

- The design shall be an exact duplicate of the quarter dollars
- Diameter of 3.0 inches
- Weight 5.0 ounces
- Contain .999 fine silver
- Incused into the edge the fineness and weight of the bullion coin (.999 Fine Silver 5.0 ounce)
- Bear an inscription of the denomination ("which shall be 'quarter dollar'")
- Not to be minted or issued by the U.S. Mint as so-called 'fractional' bullion coins

By giving it a definition in Section 5112 of Title 31 of the U.S. Code, and defining it as a coin that the treasury chief may issue, that makes it a United States coin under section 5103—the legal tender provision of the law.

The practical effect would be also to tamper with products of other coins which are "supersized" and presently do not violate counterfeiting laws, but just might under a system with silver national park five-ouncers in the mix. Here's how and why:

In recent times, a number of private manufacturers have produced large, oversized medallion-like pieces, which are replicas of contemporary coin designs. They are not intended as counterfeits, or even eye-fooling replicas, because of their size (generally over three inches in diameter—a size the Secret Service has traditionally said is not viable as a counterfeit).

Throughout the summer, fall and the campaign season, the Senate had the bill and did nothing. It took the "lame duck" Congress, post election, and the need to bail out the nation's automakers to find the time for the bill. In almost any other Congress, it would have died.

On December 10, 2008, the bill was discharged from committee, put on the unanimous consent calendar, passed, and cleared for the White House.

The legislation then went to President Bush for signature, requiring the Treasury Secretary, in consultation with the Secretary of the Interior, the chief executive of each state or territory, and other appropriate Federal officials, to choose the complete list within 270 days of enactment.

List of National Parks Designated for Coinage

YEAR	JURISDIC-TION	SITE	LEGAL AUTH.	DATE	FED. ENTITY	REL. DATE
2010	Arkansas	Hot Springs National Park	4 Stat. 505	04/20/1832	NPS	04/19/10
	Wyoming	Yellowstone National Park	17 Stat. 32	03/01/1872	NPS	06/01/10
	California	Yosemite National Park	26 Stat. 650	10/01/1890	NPS	07/26/10
	Arizona	Grand Canyon National Park	27 Stat. 469	02/20/1893	NPS	09/20/10
	Oregon	Mt. Hood National Forest	28 Stat. 1240	09/28/1893	USFS	11/15/10
2011	Pennsylvania	Gettysburg National Military Park	28 Stat. 651	02/11/1895	NPS	01/24/11
	Montana	Glacier National Park	29 Stat. 907	02/22/1897	NPS	04/04/11
	Washington	Olympic National Park	29 Stat. 901	02/22/1897	NPS	06/13/11
	Mississippi	Vicksburg National Military Park	30 Stat. 841	02/21/1899	NPS	08/29/11
	Oklahoma	Chickasaw National Recreation Area	32 Stat. 641	07/01/1902	NPS	11/14/11

YEAR	JURISDIC-TION	SITE	LEGAL AUTH.	DATE	FED. ENTITY	REL. DATE
2012	Puerto Rico	El Yunque National Forest	32 Stat. 2029	01/17/1903	USFS	
	New Mexico	Chaco Culture National Historical Park	35 Stat. 2119	03/11/1907	NPS	
	Maine	Acadia National Park	39 Stat. 1785	07/08/1916	NPS	
	Hawaii	Hawai'i Volcanoes National Park	39 Stat. 432	08/01/1916	NPS	
	Alaska	Denali National Park	39 Stat. 938	02/26/1917	NPS	
2013	New Hampshire	White Mountain National Forest	40 Stat. 1779	05/16/1918	USFS	
	Ohio	Perry's Victory and International Peace Memorial	40 Stat. 1322	03/03/1919	NPS	
	Nevada	Great Basin National Park	42 Stat. 2260	01/24/1922	NPS	
	Maryland	Fort McHenry National Monument and Historic Shrine	43 Stat. 1109	03/03/1925	NPS	
	South Dakota	Mount Rushmore National Memorial	43 Stat.1214	03/03/1925	NPS	
2014	Tennessee	Great Smoky Mountains National Park	44 Stat. 616	05/22/1926	NPS	
	Virginia	Shenandoah National Park	44 Stat. 616	05/22/1926	NPS	
	Utah	Arches National Park	46 Stat. 2988	04/12/1929	NPS	
	Idaho	Great Sand Dunes National Park	47 Stat. 2506	03/17/1932	NPS	
	Florida	Everglades National Park	48 Stat. 816	05/30/1934	NPS	
2015	Nebraska	Homestead National Monument of America	49 Stat. 1184	03/19/1936	NPS	
	Louisiana	Kisatchie National Forest	49 Stat. 3520	06/03/1936	USFS	
	North Carolina	Blue Ridge Parkway	49 Stat. 2041	06/30/1936	NPS	

YEAR	JURISDIC-TION	SITE	LEGAL AUTH.	DATE	FED. ENTITY	REL. DATE
2016	Delaware	Bombay Hook National Wildlife Refuge	45 Stat. 1222	06/22/1937	US F&W	
	New York	Saratoga National Historical Park	52 Stat. 608	06/01/1938	NPS	
	Illinois	Shawnee National Forest	54 Stat. 2649	09/06/1939	USFS	
	Kentucky	Cumberland Gap National Historical Park	54 Stat. 262	06/11/1940	NPS	
	West Virginia	Harpers Ferry National Historical Park	58 Stat. 645	06/30/1944	NPS	
	North Dakota	Theodore Roosevelt National Park	56 Stat. 326	02/25/1946	NPS	
2017	South Carolina	Fort Moultrie (Fort Sumter National Monument)	62 Stat. 204	04/28/1948	NPS	
	Iowa	Effigy Mounds National Monument	64 Stat. A371	10/25/1949	NPS	
	District of Columbia	Frederick Douglass National Historic Site	76 Stat. 435	09/05/1962	NPS	
	Missouri	Ozark National Scenic Riverways	78 Stat. 608	08/27/1964	NPS	
	New Jersey	Ellis Island National Monument (Statue of Liberty)	79 Stat. 1490	05/11/1965	NPS	
	Indiana	George Rogers Clark National Historical Park	80 Stat. 325	07/23/1966	NPS	
2018	Michigan	Pictured Rocks National Lakeshore	80 Stat. 922	10/15/1966	NPS	
	Wisconsin	Apostle Islands National Lakeshore	84 Stat. 880	09/26/1970	NPS	
	Minnesota	Voyageurs National Park	84 Stat. 1970	01/08/1971	NPS	
	Georgia	Cumberland Island National Seashore	86 Stat. 1066	10/23/1972	NPS	

YEAR	JURISDIC- TION	SITE	LEGAL AUTH.	DATE	FED. ENTITY	REL. DATE
2019	Rhode Island	Block Island National Wildlife Refuge	62 Stat. 240	04/12/1973	US F&W	
	Massa- chusetts	Lowell National Historical Park	92 Stat. 291	06/05/1978	NPS	
	Northern Mariana Islands	American Memorial Park	92 Stat. 487	08/18/1978	NPS	
	Guam	War in the Pacific National Historical Park	92 Stat. 487	08/18/1978	NPS	
	Texas	San Antonio Missions National Historical Park	92 Stat. 3636	11/10/1978	NPS	
2020	Idaho	Frank Church River of No Return Wilderness	94 Stat. 948	07/23/1980	USFS	
	American Samoa	National Park of American Samoa	102 Stat. 2879	10/31/1988	NPS	
	Connecticut	Weir Farm National Historic Site	104 Stat. 1171	10/31/1990	NPS	
	U.S. Virgin Islands	Salt River Bay National Historical Park and Ecological Preserve	106 Stat. 33	02/24/1992	NPS	
	Vermont	Marsh-Billings- Rockefeller National Historical Park	106 Stat. 934	08/26/1992	NPS	
	Kansas	Tallgrass Prairie National Preserve	110 Stat. 4204	11/12/1996	NPS	
2021	Alabama	Tuskegee Airmen National Historic Site	112 Stat. 3247	11/06/1998	NPS	

Key: NPS is National Park Service. USFS is U.S. Forest Service. USF&W is U.S. Fish and Wildlife.

Chapter Four
Will the Series have a 57th Coin
...or a 114th?

WHEN CONGRESS AND THE PRESIDENT joined forces on Dec. 23, 2008 to honor the National Park System and the National Trust for Historic Preservation with a new series of coins, they created an homage to national forests and sites within the National Wildlife Refuge System and the National Register of Historic Places. It was, perhaps, more than they intended.

The law is specific in that it covers the 50 states (where Delaware alone lacks a national park), the District of Columbia, and five named insular territories that include the Commonwealth of Puerto Rico, Guam, American Samoa, the U.S. Virgin Islands and the Commonwealth of Northern Marianas Islands.

Nothing should be clearer than the intent of the law's sponsors to produce either 56 coin designs, or 112, if the alternative that allows the Secretary of the Treasury to decree there should be a second round to benefit an entirely different group of historic sites, making it into a 20-year program—the longest in history.

However, a strong case can be made that the language of the new law makes it a 57-coin program (or a 114-coin alternative)—the 50 states, Washington, D.C., the five insular territories and the Trust Territory of the Pacific Islands—the 57th coin.

The Trust Territory of the Pacific Islands, whose origins began as the United Nations trust territory in Micronesia in the western Pacific Ocean, consist of at least four components. Administered by the United States since July 18, 1947, its members are originally a League of Nations mandate administered by Japan and taken by the United States in 1944. They are all part of a Compact of Free Association (November 3, 1986) and an Amended Compact that entered into force in May, 2004.

A unique section, 102, of the new law calls for "the Redesign and Issuance of Quarter Dollars Emblematic of National Sites in Each State, the District of Columbia, and Each Territory," and the subsequent subsection offers a unique definition "Inclusion of the District of Columbia and Territories. For purposes of this subsection, the term 'State' has the same meaning as in section 3(a)(3) of the Federal Deposit Insurance Act."

This differs from the language utilized in the legislation, which created the extension for the State Quarters Program to include Washington D.C. and the insular territories. The specific language was as follows: "For purposes of this subsection, the term 'territory' means the Commonwealth of Puerto Rico, Guam, American Samoa, the United States Virgin Islands and the Commonwealth of the Northern Mariana Islands."

Flag of the Trust Territory of the Pacific Islands.

Presumably, the words "District of Columbia" are sufficiently well-established as to not require further explanation.

Most consumers are familiar with the FDIC because it is the federal agency that governs insured deposits at banking institutions. Less well-known is just how broadly based its cushion is, and that goes with enabling legislation found in Title 12 of the United States Code, Section §1813(a)(3).

This section gives an entirely different meaning to the word "state," namely "any State of the United States, the District of Columbia, any territory of the United States, Puerto Rico, Guam, American Samoa, the Trust Territory of the Pacific Islands, the Virgin Islands, and the Northern Mariana Islands."

Notice one significant difference: use of the phrase "the Trust Territory of the Pacific Islands," not otherwise defined. Complicating the matter further: the historical note in Title 48 of the U.S. Code Annotated, which covers the Pacific Trust Territories. The note speaks of the past, even though FDIC regulations covering them lay in the future.

"With the entry into effect of the Compact with Palau, the Trusteeship of the Pacific Islands was terminated. See Proclamations of President Reagan (Proc. No. 5564, Nov. 3, 1986, 51 F.R. 40399) and President Clinton (Proc. No. 6726, Sept. 27, 1994, 59 F.R. 49777)."

Federated States of Micronesia that make up the Pacific Trust Territories consist of four states: Chuuk (Truk), Kosrae (Kosaie), Pohnpei (Ponape), and Yap. Of these, the stone money of Yap is familiar to many numismatists.

Taken literally, it is possible to argue that not only should there be a "Federated States of Micronesia" coin—the coinage for the "Trust Territory of the Pacific Islands"—but for each component of the trust territory as well.

Aerial view of Saipan, Northern Mariana Islands.
Photo by P Miller

It becomes more complicated because of the language in the new law calls for national parks, national forests, sites within the National Wildlife Refuge System and those on the National Register of Historic Places—any national site—to be given consideration as part of the design process.

National site (a separately defined word) means it is "under the supervision, management or conservancy of the National Park Service, the United States Forest Service, the United States Fish and Wildlife Service, or any similar department or agency of the Federal Government, including any national park, national monument, national battlefield, national military park, national historical park, national historic site, national lakeshore, seashore, recreation area, parkway, scenic river, or trail and any site in the National Wildlife Refuge System."

What does that translate to? There are 548 national wildlife refuges in all 50 states. Rocky Flats in Colorado was established as the 548th National Wildlife Refuge on July 12, 2007, adding nearly 4,000 acres to the refuge system.

Design proposal for the Everglades National Park quarter.
Art rendering courtesy Danbury Mint

There are also 37 Wetland Management Districts in the Prairie Pothole region of the northern Great Plains. The next surprise: The Pacific Remote Islands National Wildlife Refuge Complex is a group of unorganized, unincorporated—or in the case of Palmyra Atoll, incorporated—American Pacific Island territories managed by the Fish and Wildlife Service of the United States Department of the Interior.

The most elementary rule in drafting legislation is to be repetitive and don't make changes unless it's necessary. The presumption, therefore, is that by choosing a reference to the FDIC the drafter understood the consequences of the change and intended a much larger program than many originally thought.

Since there were no hearings held on this matter or more explanatory material provided, we are left to conclude the program scope has been altered, and America may become the coin minter to the world. We'll just have to wait and see how it winds up.

Chapter Five
Selecting National Parks and Designs

AMERICA'S BEAUTIFUL NATIONAL PARKS QUARTER Dollar Coin Act of 2008 provided formal guidelines for choosing national parks and their respective coin designs.

Site selection process:

Step 1

The U.S. Mint will initiate the site selection process by contacting the chief executive of each host jurisdiction (State/District of Columbia/Territory) through a formal letter of request to identify one preferred and three ranked alternative national sites in his or her jurisdiction. The U. S. Mint will provide resources and access to lists of applicable national sites to each chief executive. National sites for consideration include any site under the supervision, management, or conservancy of the National Park Service, the United States Forest Service, the United States Fish and Wildlife Service, or any similar department or agency of the Federal government.

Step 2

With due consideration to the requirement that the national site chosen for each host jurisdiction shall be the most appropriate in terms of natural and historic significance, and after giving full and thoughtful consideration to national sites that are not under the jurisdiction of the Secretary of the Interior, the chief executive will provide the U.S. Mint his or her recommendation for the national site to be honored on the respective quarter, as well as three recommended alternative national sites in order of preference.

Step 3

The U.S. Mint will review all the recommendations and will establish a candidate list of the 56 national sites.

Step 4

The U.S. Mint will consult with the Secretary of the Interior to ensure appropriateness of each of the 56 national site recommendations based on their natural or historic significance, and to validate the date on which each recommended site was established as a national site.

Step 5

Having consulted with each chief executive and the Secretary of the Interior, and having given full and thoughtful consideration to national sites that are not under the jurisdiction of the Secretary of the Interior, the U. S. Mint will reconcile all comments and recommend a final candidate list determined to be the most appropriate in terms of natural and historic significance to the Secretary of the Treasury, who will approve the final national site list. The approved list will also establish the order in which each quarter-dollar is released. Quarter-dollars will be released at a rate of five per year beginning in 2010.

The designs are then vetted by the Commission of Fine Arts ("CFA"), established by Act of Congress in 1910, and also by the Citizens Coinage Advisory Committee, established by Congress in 2003. (The Mission and Purpose of the CCAC set forth by Public Law 108-15 is to advise the Secretary of the Treasury on the themes and designs of all U.S. coins and medals. The CCAC serves as an informed, experienced and impartial resource to the Secretary of the Treasury and represents the interests of American citizens and collectors).

Vetting of the coins got started in the fall of 2009; a 34-page transcript of the September 17, 2009 meeting of the Commission of Fine Arts began with the Mint trying to explain the program and the CFA members challenging the notion that millions of acres of land, scenery and history could fit in a planchet just 24.3mm in diameter.

Commissioners present for the hearing included Earl A. Powell III, Chair; Pamela Nelson, Vice-chair; Diana Balmori; John Belle; Elizabeth Plater-Zyberk; and Witold Rybczynski, who began with a statement as well as a question:

Mr. Rybczynski: *Yosemite on a quarter.*
Ms. Nelson: *It is very hard to get the Grand Canyon on a quarter.*
Mr. Rybczynski: *Did somebody think of that?*
Ms. Balmori: *Well, there are some good artists who could ... "*

The first discussion was the obverse or face side of the coin. The Mint offered this analysis:

"So we will start with the obverse. The obverse will feature the familiar restored 1932 portrait of George Washington by John Flanagan including subtle details and the beauty of the original model. The inscriptions are 'United States of America,' 'Liberty,' 'In God We

Trust,' and 'Quarter Dollar.'"

There was some questioning of what was being done to the design. "Notice there is quite a difference in the hair. The hair is much more refined. Some people call it kind of spaghetti hair in the past years, so we are bringing back that more subtle sculptural detail in this model.

Ms. Balmori: *That is a good one.*
Ms. Nelson: *Very nice.*
Mr. Luebke: *He did. Now he has got camel hair or something."*

The discussion then went to the reverse (found with each coin in the text below).

What the Mint wanted to do was set different parameters than the 50 State Quarters Program had, and they did that by managing the

Members of the Commission of Fine Arts, February 2009. Standing, L to R, Elizabeth Plater-Zyberk, Witold Rybczynski, N. Michael McKinnell, John Belle. Seated, L to R, Pamela Nelson, Vice Chairman Earl A. Powell III, Chairman Diana Balmori.

template of the coin given to the artists and the states. That initiated some dialogue as well:

"I just wanted to mention also about the template. It was designed for the reverse with a circular, recessed base with the inscriptions along the outer rim. The central design will be sculpted above the recessed circular base, and the name of the national site is featured at the top. The template supports a new sculptural design and consistency for all designs throughout the duration of the program."

Ms. Nelson: *So this is starting with the direction of the consistent template for all the designs.*
Ms. Budow: *Correct. We wanted to have it distinguished from the 50 State Quarters Program and have a new look.*
Ms. Balmori: *Is there one artist for all of them? Or what? How is this being done?*
Ms. Budow: *Oh, no. There are multiple artists. They all use the same*

template, but all the designs were done by different artists. A number of artists worked on the project.

Ms. Balmori: *What are the bases of their designs? Are they using photographs of this, of the parks?*

Ms. Budow: *We worked very closely with the superintendents of the particular sites, Hot Springs and Grand Canyon, et cetera, and they informed us as to which designs they thought would be most emblematic and appropriate to be on the coin and then photographs to support those designs. So, yes; they were primarily based on photographs. And we took a lot of, like I said, guidance from the superintendents' offices as to what they thought was most important in honoring that site on the quarter.*

So it is a little bit different from the process in the 50 State Quarters Program."

And so it was, also, with the Citizens Coinage Advisory Committee that met on Sept. 22, 2009 in Washington. Attending were John Alexander Doreen Bolger, Michael Brown, Arthur Houghton, Gary Marks, Rick Meier, Mitch Sanders (Chairperson), Donald Scarinci and Joe Winter (via telephone).

Citizens Coinage Advisory Committee member Gary Marks examines a sketch of a proposed coin design.
Photo courtesy Donald Scarinci

Their complaint about the obverse was that it used George Washington at all, as their minutes reveal "several members expressed disappointment that the committee's recommendation to portray Theodore Roosevelt on the quarter's obverse for the duration of the America the Beautiful Quarters Program was not implemented. U.S. Mint staff explained to the committee that in the absence of any mandate for change from the Secretary of the Treasury or the U.S. Congress, the existing obverse design (in a modified version) was retained."

The CCAC members set forth the way that they would evaluate each design: they would "rate proposed designs by assigning 0, 1, 2 or 3 points to each, with higher points reflecting more favorable evaluations. With nine members present and voting, the maximum possible point total was 27."

By the fall of 2011, the Commission on Fine Arts set its agenda to deal with 2013 designs for the America the Beautiful Quarters Program. The minutes expand on this: "Ms. Cynthia Vitelli summarized the authorizing legislation for the series of 56 reverses for the circulating quarter-dollar coins, corresponding to national sites in each of the U.S. states and territories. The current submission includes alternative designs for the five reverses to be issued in 2013. She noted the continuing portrait of George Washington on the obverse, with restoration of the original detailing of the sculpting by John Flanagan in the early 1930s; the Commission members expressed support for this restoration effort. She also noted that the Mint consults with the superintendent of each federal site to develop inspiration for the designs and ensure that they are historically accurate and emblematic of the location."

But their view on Fort McHenry was less successful as far as the Mint was concerned. Bill McAllister, formerly of the *Washington Post*, now a *Coin World* correspondent, quotes CFA chair Earl A. Powell III as saying the four Mint designs were "more about soldiers than forts." Powell's suggestion: the Mint should consider an aerial view of the Baltimore fort's unique design.

The three proposed designs for Ohio's Perry's Victory and International Peace Memorial were also rejected as "problematic," which is expressed more harshly in the transcript. The Fine Arts transcript and minutes are impressive in their passion and criticism; the Mint version before the Citizens meeting takes the passion and makes it into pablum, which is a shame for those who view this process historically.

Cynthia Meals Vitelli, who presented at the Commission of Fine Arts for the Mint, promised to relay their concerns to Mint officials.

THE EVOLUTION of the Citizens Coinage Advisory Committee is a remarkable one, owing in no small measure to the earlier Citizens Commemorative Coin Advisory Committee. How the Mint learned to deal with outside committees was highly beneficial to the design process and the overall America the Beautiful Program.

It was evident to some of the citizens that even with the "artistic infusion" program introduced by Mint director Henrietta Fore, and expanded by her successor, Edmund Moy, that the designers were muddling through on some issues. The view of some was that the designs were pedestrian and incapable of being award-winning in any sense of the word.

Citizens Coinage Advisory Committee, meeting. Acting U.S. Mint Director, Richard Peterson showing plans for the proposed new space for mint artists to work at the Philadelphia Mint to CCAC members Heidi Wastweet, Erik Jansen, Gary Marks. A better work space for the artists was a recommendation in the CCAC's report to improve America's coin designs, issued in 2010.
Photo courtesy Donald Scarinci

By the November 29, 2011 meeting, CCAC members took the bull by the horns and excoriated some of the designs presented by the Mint for the America the Beautiful Coin Program. As reported by Bill McAllister in *Coin World*, committee member Donald Scarinci was particularly infuriated by the pedestrian nature of the designs offered for Ohio.

"Let's establish this. You blew it on this one," Scarinci said. "There is nothing artistic here. Nobody could think anything is good here."

Whether the Mint can adopt constructive criticism and takes a different approach in the future remains to be seen, but it is clear that there are some—at least on the Citizens Committee—committed to artistic excellence.

Chapter Six
Grading National Park State Quarters

GRADING NATIONAL PARK STATE QUARTERS is similar to grading any other coin of modern mintage. There is the design on the front or obverse of George Washington, updated from its 1932 glory—executed by John Flanagan—and the thoroughly modern reverse designs that depict an aspect of the national park being commemorated. Then there is the third side of the coin, its edge, which has to be examined in the state park series because of its edge lettering and the sheer size on the three-inch, five-ounce coin that is gigantic in every respect. (The edge is 3.25mm in width; the circumference of the three-inch coin is about 9.4 inches in overall length.

The working surface of the edge of the coin is far larger than that which typically goes into the hands of the engraver. This is similar to an art medal, and the large-sized coins in particular are difficult to grade because the large surface area magnifies rather than absorbs minor flaws.

1932 coin is emulated by the new series. Which design is better is a matter of taste.

There are general rules for grading coins that apply to the national park coinage—those that are in circulation and proof specimens. These regulations generally have nothing to do with the mystery or excitement of detailing the design, but rather, having now made the cut, it's to try and give collectors and investors good value for one's money.

There are some interesting points on the new coin, but nothing is more interesting or telling than the fractional inch of a diameter on the rim, which is the part of the coin that virtually no one has learned how to grade because, until recently, reeded-edge coinage was all there was.

You can learn in five minutes how to grade the obverse. The high points on the coin are at the end of Washington's powdered wig and around his ear lobes. These areas will show weakness, as will the evident crease at the chin-line. Also, the field off Washington's nose and behind his head curls are also prone to contact marks.

U.S. Mint, 88 Fifth Street, San Francisco, California
Photo by Mike Hofmann

When you look at a coin to grade it, hold it by the edge—very carefully—not ever on the face or national park design side.

The five-ounce coins will grade differently than the 24-millimeter counterparts, and many (it appears) will stay in a plastic holder, meaning that how these coins are struck at the mint will be the determining factor. But all of this has to be seen in context and compared with the way other coins are graded (and eventually priced).

Here's a quick primer for those who have started collecting coins, or investing in them, with this series. These comments are not meant to make you into a world-class grader but are intended to provide general guidance as you acquire coins and then seek out the best of the best for your collection.

Although you may have read about how precise coin grading is, or seen it in advertisements, or eBay offers and seen how exacting grading descriptions appear (e.g., "Mint State-65 [uncirculated]"), coin grading in fact is an imprecise but necessary adjunct of collecting coins or investing in them. Grading is both descriptive of a physical condition and serves as a basis for price.

To understand the numerical grading system, it helps to visualize a

12-inch ruler, with the numbers running from left to right. Generically, "good" is at the left end, perhaps at the one-inch mark, and refers to well-worn coins of the type that had served as pocket change for a substantial period of time. The "fine" coin is in the middle, perhaps at the six-inch mark; its design elements are all quite clear, but it, too, has been in circulation. The typical so-called uncirculated coin falls at the 10-inch mark and still has its mint sheen, without a lot of contact marks on its surface. From 10 to 12 inches on the ruler are the other, "better" grades of uncirculated coins.

Based on examining the surface of the coin's metal, and focusing on such factors as eye appeal, the strength of the strike, and the luster or sheen that time has given the piece, coin grading seeks to evaluate the state of preservation and relative condition of a particular coin, and ultimately offers an opinion to its value.

Design proposal for the Cumberland Island National Park quarter.
Art rendering courtesy Danbury Mint

Generally, coins are either uncirculated, or not (i.e., circulated). But "uncirculated" is an ill-defined term, since by the time it is in your hands it is literally in circulation.

Coin grading is characterized by the lack of a single fixed, definitive standard, but for those with an appreciation for the fact that other things in life are compared and priced based on sensory factors, coin grading is not unlike the comparing fine wines or edible beef (cattle). (Robert Parker pioneered the 1-to-100 grading scale in his publication *The Wine Advocate*, yet others use a 1-to-20 scale, and some prefer alphabetical (A, B+, B, and so forth).

Coins are widely graded in one of two ways: numerically or adjectivally. Adjectives, and even numbers alone, cannot adequately convey what is unavoidably a subjective impression, although many try to ignore this inherent limitation. Some cataloguers grade by comparison—but if the "best" example of a piece known to a grader, cataloguer, or collector changes, so inevitably do all comparisons based on it.

Given the overwhelmingly subjective nature of coin grading, it is not surprising that there have been many known examples of the same coin being graded differently over time. This is not necessarily true for America the Beautiful coins, but it certainly could be—especially with the large-sized models.

1870-CC Double Eagle (reverse): This AU-graded coin is "born circulated."
Photo courtesy Heritage

One of my favorite examples is a rare 1870-CC Double Eagle or $20 gold piece that was sold at auction by three different firms at three different times. Each cataloguer agreed that the coin was "finest known," but one called it about uncirculated (AU) and the other two termed it extremely fine (XF).

That experienced graders or cataloguers can disagree on coins does not seem to be unusual, though it can be problematic.

Numerical grading originated with the 1958 publication by Dr. William Sheldon of *Penny Whimsy* (also known as *Early American Cents 1793-1814*), a book that attempted to quantify as well as qualify the grading of large cents. Dr. Sheldon devised a scale based on numbers one through 70, which were intended to roughly correlate with some of the adjectival descriptions. However, unlike the adjectives, which referred to wear, Dr. Sheldon's methodology was originally specifically geared to price. For example, a coin in Fine-12 condition was assumed to be equivalent to one-fifth the price of an Uncirculated-60 coin, even though the wear on the coin was nowhere nearly as substantial as the numbers might suggest.

The natural focus of texts, periodicals and litigation is on gradations within the uncirculated classification, not only because that is where most of the value lies, but also because those are the gradations most difficult to see, articulate and describe.

Q. David Bowers, who is a famous coin dealer, outstanding researcher, author of dozens of books about coins, and cataloguer of hundreds of auctions over the last half century, offers this intriguing observation:

"Often five different sellers will assign five different grades to the same coin, perhaps differing just slightly but still differing, often with important financial consequences. As the evaluation of the grade or condition of a coin is a largely subjective matter, experts can legitimately differ."

Occasionally, a lawsuit is brought, and in one case brought by the Federal Trade Commission the Court tried to explain the difference in various grading opinions.

"The value of a rare coin depends on its condition. In evaluating a coin's condition or 'grade,' a number of factors are considered, including: (1) the coin's overall appearance and eye appeal; (2) the number of marks and scratches it has; (3) its toning, color and tarnish; and (4) its 'strike' or the clarity of the impression made in the minting process.

Renowned numismatist Q. David Bowers.
Photo courtesy Donn Pearlman for Professional Numismatists Guild, Inc.

"Different grading systems and individual graders may weigh these factors differently in grading coins. Thus, for example, some graders may be more strict about overall eye appeal, while others give more emphasis to the amount of rubbing and bag marks."

According to the Court's analysis, "The grading of coins is an art, not a science, and always involves a certain amount of subjectivity. In addition, grading standards have changed over the years."

But a one to 70 scale remains confusing to those who become newly interested or casually interested in collecting, where an A, B, C, D, E and F scale, or one to 100, is instantly translatable from academic experience to the real world. (An "A" or "90" or above is of really superior quality, just as it is on a test in school).

Today, there are professional grading services that can assist the novice, or even the most advanced collector. But grading of rare coins, even with professional services doing the bulk of the work on expensive, hard-to-grade items, still hasn't solved the issue that the description of a coin remains more of an art than a science.

Excellent text books such as a Jim Halperin's *NCI Grading Guide*, and the *Official PCGS Grading Guide*, edited by Scott Travers, go a long way toward making the process scientific—and actually can teach reliable techniques that collectors, investors and dealers can consistently use.

Chapter Seven
Valuation and How Silver Influences the Process

THOUGH THE HEADLINES this past year belonged to gold, by far the bigger story was the unprecedented gain over the past three years for silver, which had a cumulative compounded gain of about 36.5 percent annually. Even with sell-offs, the gain was impressive and had an impact on all bullion items ranging from the one-ounce American silver eagle to the five-ounce, three-inch diameter America the Beautiful coin (ATB is the shorthand widely used). The frenzy in the precious metal markets led to unprecedented demand for bullion coins.

Silver options trading pit at the Commodity Exchange in New York.
Photo courtesy David Mark

Moreover, Congress, seeking a niche market, authorized the Mint to produce two separate silver coin varieties: first was a silver quarter weighing .0739 troy ounces and 24.3mm in diameter, while the second was a unique five-ounce, three-inch diameter coin that is identical in design with the circulation model, right down to its legal tender worth of 25 cents—even though its precious metal content far exceeds its stated value.

Here's the contrast between the two identically designed silver-issue coins except for size and weight:

DIAMETER	WEIGHT (troy oz)	VALUE AT $28/oz
24.3mm (.96 in)	.0739	$2
76.4mm (3.0 in)	5.0	$140

So for each of these legal tender 25-cent coins, there's really a coin worth much more than face value.

Indeed, the large coin contains about $140 worth of silver. It's being offered by the Mint to the public as "proof-like" bullion with a selling price to the public at around $239—about $99 over its intrinsic value. Still, demand continues to be very strong. ATB coins are off to the races!

Through the years, silver coins and silver bullion have been an important component of many collectors' and investors' portfolios. Some common-date silver coins have had more value as a bullion-like item than for its numismatic worth.

As former Mint director Philip Diehl points out in the Preface: Oh, to be a fly on the wall a millennium from now when a numismatist from the 31st century compares the small silver coin with the identical (except size and weight) large one! Surely, he will scratch his head trying to figure out just how we used precious metals with regard to our physical currency.

Silver in World History

A clear understanding of the large, five-ounce ATB coin can only be seen in the context of silver's historical role during ancient and colonial times. In the beginning, according to the Bible's Book of Genesis (13:2), the wealth of a patriarch later known as Abraham is described as being "very rich in cattle, in silver, and in gold."

The earliest known of all precious metal circulating coinage—that of Lydia (circa 750 B.C.), what is now western Turkey—was made from electrum, a natural alloy of gold and silver combined.

Silver was traded by weight, in a unit of weight called shekels, starting around 3,000 B.C., but the marking of the electrum coinage in Lydia is what truly began the rise of silver as both a method of payment and an early investment.

Far more plentiful than gold, silver was first mined in western Turkey, but the Greeks elevated mining to an art form at Laurium, not far from modern day Athens. From about 600 B.C. to 300 B.C., the Laurium mines probably produced about a million ounces of silver a year, according to the Silver Institute.

Later, there were mines in Spain that, for nearly a millennium, produced enough silver to satisfy, first, the needs of the Roman Empire, then Carthage, and ultimately southern Germany and the Austro-Hungarian Empire.

Most estimates today say that from the Laurium era, 600 to 300 B.C., mining operations totaled about 900,000 ounces of silver each year. About 273 million ounces were produced during this era.

Just as the Spanish, South German and Hungarian mines were diminishing in their silver production, a New World was discovered by the voyages of exploration. Given that one purpose of their journeys was the riches of gold and silver, they succeeded beyond their wildest expectations.

Silver was the first metal discovered by the Conquistadores in New Spain, making good on the investment of King Ferdinand and Queen Isabella. A fleet of vessels looted South and Central American silver mines, filling the coffers in Madrid.

By the mid-1530s, a Casa de Moneda, or mint, had been built in Mexico City—the first in the New World—to support the rapidly growing Spanish empire. A determination was made that the New World would give

Electrum coinage of Lydia (modern day Turkey), circa 750 B.C.

up its bounty to the Royal Treasury of Castille, which the Spaniards did, striking 38mm silver coins commonly called pieces of eight—the first currency widely accepted worldwide.

Three centralized locations and good Spanish records suggest that Mexico produced about 1.5 billion troy ounces of silver between 1500-1800; that the Potosi region of Bolivia also produced around 1.5 billion troy ounces to complement Mexico. And Peru, from about 1600 to 1800, averaged three million ounces a year or 600 million ounces, taking us to the cusp of the 19th century when the American discovery of the Comstock Lode created a disorderly displacement in the precious metals market.

History of Silver Mining Production

PRIMARY SOURCE/ERA	YEARS	TOTAL PROD. (million troy oz)
Laurium (Greek) era	600 to 300 B.C	273
Roman Empire to Early Middle Ages	300 B.C to 600 A.D.	1,350
Middle Ages	600 to 1400	2
World	1400 to 1600	747
World	1601 to 1700	1,272
World	1701 to 1800	1,833
World	1801 to 1900	5,099
World	1901 to 1927	5,406
World	1928 to 1940	1,755
World	1941 to 2010	124,566
	TOTAL	142,303

The total silver produced from the dawn of history until 2012, using latest statistics available, is about 142,303-million troy ounces. It is mined in 58 countries, including Mexico, the United States and Canada.

By contrast, in January, 2009, *National Geographic* estimated only about 161,000 metric tons of gold had been produced in world history—just less than the size of two Olympic-size swimming pools. All told, about 24 times more silver than gold has been mined.

Silver in American History

In the late 18th century, gold and silver metal, bullion, foreign coin or plate could be deposited with the Mint where, for a small service or convenience fee, the Mint would melt it down and coin it into national money using prescribed weights and sizes. The value of gold and silver per ounce was determined, the volume of metal legislated, and coinage was ready as soon as the Mint director and chief coiner filed their bonds—which took about two years to process.

Each gold coin had its full weight and measure, that is, a gold eagle had just about $10 worth of gold in it. Silver dollars were similarly regulated, as were subsidiary coinage, but the historic problem is that precious metal prices are generally unstable absent a market-maker who guarantees a fixed price.

As a result, American silver coinage was worth more melted than coined. Deposits all but ceased, coinage flowed abroad to settle debts or for melting, and by the turn of the 19th century, silver dollar coinage was entirely suspended—not to be restarted until the mid-1830s. Nowadays, virtually all American coinage minted before the 1830s is scarce, even if its stated mintage seems high.

Lacking a domestic source of gold, until deposits were discovered decades later in the Carolinas and Georgia, there wasn't much gold coinage either. (The gold rush in California and Alaska lay in the future.)

Through the early 1800s, there was a real need for coinage, and Congress continually tried to rectify the problem by regulating the value of foreign coins that circulated domestically. (The number of foreign coins that could be used and were accepted is astonishing; the confusion in pricing—each had a different value—at retail establishments is difficult for a 21st century reader to imagine.)

Treasury Secretary William Windom

Unlike other nations whose coinage was periodically removed from circulation, or made illegal to own or use, with the notable exception of a gold recall in the 1930s and several attempts to ban melting, all U.S. coins were—and remain to this day—a legal tender for all debts, public or private. You can offer any coin, and it cannot be refused.

More than a century ago, Attorney General MacVeagh, in an 1881 opinion to Treasury Secretary William Windom on redemption of national bank notes, states it succinctly: "The government notes are promises to pay in dollars; for such promises, the thing promised may properly be substituted by the promisor."

When the new golden presidential dollars came out, I took a used trade dollar (1877-S), worth about $150, and tendered it with

19 Federal Reserve notes to a U.S. Mint employee at Grand Central terminal in New York City, the site where the Mint staged a major public relations event.

Though it took a supervisor or two—who all tried to persuade me that the trade dollar had numismatic value far exceeding is face worth—the Mint finally exchanged it for a presidential golden dollar, proving the legal tender property remained.

Citizens under the earliest elements of this system had the right to deposit silver or gold bullion with the Mint and receive, in return, a full measure of precious metal coinage, less the cost of coining. The government and the population could, thus, control currency supplies. The right to deposit these metals was called "free coinage," though this was hardly so since there was a modest charge by the Mint for the service.

This existed as a practice from the time that the Mint opened in 1792—when George and Martha Washington's silver plate was turned into coin—until free coinage of silver ended with passage of the Coinage Act of 1873.

Millions of ounces of silver were purchased and turned into coin, but as all of the warnings in the 1860s suggested, as the market flooded with silver, the price of the metal continued to go down. As the years progressed, the Mint bought silver, turned it into coin, received the coin back, re-coined it, and the process seemed circular. In fact, this organized melting of un-current coin makes silver dollar mintage figures meaningless; the same is true for subsidiary coinage.

Subsidiary coinage (half dollar, quarter, 20-cent piece, dime and three-cent silver coin) was produced to meet the needs of small change; silver dollars made a political statement.

The report of John Jay Knox, Deputy Comptroller of the Currency, filed a report to the Secretary of the Treasury dated April 25, 1870. It fundamentally altered the relationship and love affair that America had with silver to that point in time.

Transmitted to Congress, it resulted in the creation of a Bureau of the Mint, and while changing some aspects of the coinage law, by and large retained the underlying philosophy of the original Mint Act of 1792 in the draft legislation that would ultimately be enacted three years later.

The Coinage Act of 1873 became the cornerstone of the Mint's modern legal history. It was possible, as late as the early 1980s, to locate statutes in the then-current U.S. Code that directly quoted from language whose origin could be traced directly to the Mint Act of April 2, 1792. To be certain, there were stylistic and linguistic changes that were affected; but, for example, the Assay Commission's verbiage in 1965 was virtually identical to the Mint Act of 1792 regarding required inscriptions on modern U.S. coins.

Architect of the Coinage Act of 1873, Comptroller of the Currency John Jay Knox.

Silver in Modern Times

The discovery of silver at Nevada's Comstock Lode was an event of world monetary significance. It changed the way the nation looked at precious metals and set the standard for multiple generations of world finance. The silver lode and the gold vein at Sutter's Mill proved the allure of gold and silver from ancient times had inured to the present. But it also proved the supremacy of gold, and the beginning of a century decline in the value of silver—a metal that would not really recover its sheen until the 21st century.

The "New Deal" initiated by President Franklin Delano Roosevelt offered price support for those in the business of mining and producing silver. They needed it. From a high in 1874 of $1.29 an ounce, silver went into a shocking decline, falling to 65 cents an ounce in 1900. Incredibly, prices kept going down, sinking to a low of 24½ cents an ounce in 1933.

The 1933 Annual Report of the Director of the Mint says the Mint purchased 1.3-million ounces of silver at an average cost of 27 cents an ounce despite relatively strong demand—even in the midst of the Great Depression, silver use in the arts was estimated at 24.2-million ounces.

Acting under the Executive Proclamation of December 21, 1933, and citing the silver resolution adopted by the World Economic & Monetary Conference held in London on July 20, 1933, the Mint and assay offices of the United States were authorized over the next four years to buy domestic mined (new) silver at 64.6 cents, which, according to the 1934 Annual Report of the Director of the Mint, compared to an open market price of 43 cents.

Miners then received another boost over and above the price subsidy. A silver purchase act was approved June 19, 1934, which directed an increase in the silver monetary stock. The aim was to raise it to a quarter of the gold monetary stock.

President Roosevelt effectively nationalizes silver in 1934.
FDR Library

The 1934 Mint report characterizes what can be described as a significant change: "This act also directed issue of silver certificates against silver bullion, authorized the coinage of standard silver dollars, and authorized nationalization of silver, which was proclaimed by the President August 9, 1934." (An Office of Domestic Gold & Silver Operations was established in the Treasury Department. It would continue to function—its licensing authority finally terminated by Executive Order 11825 on December 31, 1974, and the office was finally disbanded July 31, 1975.)

Enter World War II, and there was a real need for silver again—this time as a substitute for nickel. "War nickels" were authorized by Congress on March 27, 1942 to take the place of the copper-nickel five-cent coin because copper and nickel were both critical war materials used for munitions.

The actual Act by Congress called for 50 percent silver and 50 percent copper, but gave authority for other changes if public interest warranted. To distinguish the coins further, and to allow for their eventual withdrawal from circulation later, large mintmarks labeled P, D and S were placed above the Monticello dome on the reverse.

Weight of the coin's pure silver consisted of 0.05626 troy ounces which, at 40 cents an ounce made the coins worth about 2.2 cents for their metal content. By 1961, when the Treasury stabilized the price of silver bullion at $1.29 an ounce, it made War nickels worth seven cents apiece. At the height of the 1980 boom, when the price of silver topped $48 an ounce, there was $2.70 worth of metal in each coin.

Approximately 870 million War nickels were produced from 1942 to 1945, using about 50-million ounces of silver from the strategic reserve. That same reserve was utilized until just recently to produce American bullion Eagle coins, the predecessor to the five-ounce America the Beautiful silver coinage and bullion coinage.

And so it was until the early 1960s, when, slowly, the price of silver increased, an event which would not only affect the coin industry, but also the American economy. It began innocently enough in 1961 when the price went from $.91 an ounce to $1.04. By the following year, silver had gone to a high of $1.22, and in 1963, the price hit $1.29, the level at which melting of silver coins became theoretically possible (though the actual number would be somewhat higher before it would be economically desirable).

Although the price of silver at $1.29 an ounce remained in effect continuously from September 9, 1963 to May 18, 1967, activity in the silver market precipitated a keen new interest in coins, which were seemingly destined to substantially increase in value.

Still, the anticipated boon for collectors and investors was fraught with curious setbacks. As of 1963, the Treasury Department continued to honor the contractual verbiage of silver certificates, redeeming each one for a single silver dollar. Hoards of silver certificates were redeemed on this pledge causing a virtual run on the Treasury. In the process, bags of rare silver dollars, many dated 1903 from the New Orleans Mint (1903-O), were discovered in quantity. Pieces that had been scarce plummeted virtually overnight, going from $1,500 to $30 a coin.

Mint officials wondered if there were still more old silver dollars collecting dust in their vaults and, astonishingly enough, found 2.9 million Carson City Mint silver dollars. Eventually, Congress decided that they should be auctioned, which took place in a series of four sales during the mid-1970s.

Now, nearly a half century later, many New Orleans Mint and Carson City silver dollars have yet to fully recover their old value. Nevertheless, the astute observer at the time would have noticed sales for Morgan silver dollars remained firm despite the supply glut—a harbinger of things to come.

Around this time, Nelson Bunker and his brother William Herbert Hunt began accumulating large amounts of silver. Late in the decade, the Hunt Brothers had nearly cornered the market. At its fevered pitch, between September 1979 and January 1980, silver went from

$11 to $48 an ounce. When the Hunt Brothers were unable to meet a massive margin call, prices came tumbling back down, nearly bringing down a venerable stockbrokerage in the process. But there began an attraction—silver was exciting again!

Today's robust bull market can perhaps be traced to when private gold ownership was again permitted as of December 31, 1974. Amid much fanfare, in September 1986, the Mint introduced gold bullion coins. By year's end, its silver counterpart was minted. Complete sell-outs of proof versions of both of these popular 1986-dated pieces occurred, with uncirculated sales of millions of pieces going far beyond the projections of the Mint and its private industry distributors. By 1991, tens of millions of silver coins had been issued.

Into the 21st century, with a 25-year performance record behind it, many must wonder what took the government so long to get back into the business of selling precious metals.

Beside bullion coins designed to compete with foreign products of a similar nature, and coins for circulation, which have historically been utilized by the populace as well as acquired by collectors, the U.S. Mint has produced special commemorative coins intended for collectors since 1892. That year, a silver commemorative half-dollar coin issued in honor of the 400th Anniversary of Columbus' Discovery of the New World, began a historic tradition that continued with 144 different silver coin designs on a regular basis until 1954. The practice resumed in 1981 and has proved to be highly successful. Every piece was and remains a legal tender coin, still redeemable at its face value.

More than 45 years ago, a private company then-named General Numismatics Corporation (later called the Franklin Mint) invigorated the production of foreign coinage in particular and commemorative coinage in general.

By obtaining contracts from foreign governments, its founder, Joseph Segal, and its mintmaster, former chief engraver of the United States Gilroy Roberts, created a company that proved not only could coins be produced for circulation, but a hefty profit could be made by creating and selling coins specifically designed for collectors.

The Franklin Mint also expanded the marketplace, reaching those who had never been coin collectors but could be given the insight or "itch" to acquire legal tender monies made of precious metals. The massive sales by the Franklin Mint were widely imitated.

The U.S. Mint resisted commemorative coinage programs, whenever proposed, on the same tired grounds that had been advanced from 1929 onward: They claimed that it was incompatible with circulating coinage. In 1981, however, a commemoration at the bi-sesquicentennial of the birth of George Washington was approved. Other issues followed, each approved by Congress and all manufactured and sold by the U.S. Mint.

For some brief moments, the Olympic coinage program spilled over into the front pages of the *Wall Street Journal* and other periodicals; the program's success led to others. By 1987, U.S. Mint sales to collectors and investors topped the $1-billion mark, the equivalent of a Fortune 500 company.

Thus, given, among other things, the rise in the price of precious metals, federal legislation permitting the minting of bullion coins, and the government's actual participation as a seller of such coins, it is easy to see how coin collecting rapidly grew from a small hobby to a growth industry all its own.

Former chief engraver at the U.S. Mint, Gilroy Roberts. *Photo courtesy* Coin World

Quite besides these coins, bulk silver coins in large quantities are invested in, rather than collected. The Commodity Futures Trading Commission has long had the authority to regulate transactions for delivery of gold and silver bullion pursuant to standard margin or leverage account contracts.

The Commodity Futures Trading Commission, and, indeed, the mercantile exchanges, are not concerned with legislating (nor can they legislate) small, minor purchases of one-ounce and five-ounce coins, ten-ounce bars, or numismatic items, because their statutory concern is directed toward preventing "excessive speculation" causing price fluctuations in the marketplace, which small units are incapable of creating.

What is being regulated is futures trading—the buying and selling of standardized contracts for the future delivery of a specific grade and amount of a commodity. Indeed, the legislative history refers continually to individuals or entities who can only be characterized as commodity brokers and commodity dealers, or as securities brokers and securities dealers, whose practices are regulated by the Commodity Futures Trading Commission.

Proposed IRS Regulation §1.6045-1, as published in the Federal Register on November 15, 1982, noted no intent of going beyond commodities for which there are regulated futures traded on the various commodities exchanges.

As of mid-1983 when these regulations first went into effect, the Commodity Futures Trading Commission had approved trading for the following relevant units: 100-ounce gold bars, 5000-ounce silver bars, 50-ounce platinum bars, and 100-ounce palladium bars at the Commodity Exchange (Comex), which is now a division of the New York Mercantile Exchange. Smaller lots of gold and silver, so-called "mini" contracts, units of 33.2 troy ounces (one kilo) and 1000 ounces respectively, are traded at the MidAmerica Commodity Exchange, which is affiliated with the Chicago Board of Trade. These items trade daily.

Activity in the precious metals marketplace is robust. On December 6, 2011, for example, the Comex reported silver's open interest—the number of contracts outstanding—was 95,684.

U.S. silver coins in bags of $1,000 face (without mixing denominations therein) have also been approved for trading, but are not currently traded on organized exchanges. Though bulk silver coins are not quoted any more, prices can be obtained in the *Coin Dealer Newsletter*, a respected hobby weekly price guide. There are many collectors, vest pocket dealers and investors who acquire these bags; the investment is the silver metal, but the add-on is the numismatic value.

A coin *always* remains a medium of exchange, whether its value rises or falls below a par value. For example, in 1919, the selling price of silver rose above the nominal value of American currency, when the price of silver topped $1.38 an ounce.

A silver dollar struck in 1904 or earlier contained .7734 troy ounces of silver (derived by taking the gross weight of 26.73 grams and multiplying it by the fineness, .900 fine, then dividing by the weight of one troy ounce, 31.1035 grams). The silver in the coin was worth $1.06, six cents more than face value.

There is no hint that the coins were no longer used as legal tender, or lost status as a currency, even though the government itself counts its bullion and face value when determining the nation's net worth. In fact, anecdotally, silver dollars could be acquired at East Coast banks as late as 1960; the banks would replace any silver certificate presented with a silver dollar.

The "power to 'coin money'...is a prerogative of sovereignty," and the currency of a nation is therefore evidence of its sovereignty. Congress certainly recognized this when it authorized the creation of a Mint, and in the debate which accompanied reauthorization of a mint each succeeding two years through 1828. Domestic statutes protect against counterfeiting the currency of another nation. South African Krugerrands (gold), Canadian Maple Leafs (gold and silver) and Mexican Onzas (primarily silver) are examples of those covered.

CONSIDERING HOW MUCH SILVER COIN is out there, was there a need for the America the Beautiful five-ounce silver coins? It turns out that despite billions of silver coins—even after the great coin melts of the 1960s—the overwhelming demand for the America the Beautiful five-ounce pieces validates the program.

Summary of American Silver Coinage Minted and Melted

	MINTED	MELTED	NET AVAIL	% MELTED	% AVAIL
Dollars	855,661,153	325,437,470	530,223,683	38.03	61.97
Trade Dollars	35,965,924	1,721,332	34,244,592	4.79	95.21
Half Dollars	1,790,917,250	171,608,886	1,619,308,364	9.58	90.42
Quarters	4,449,108,957	282,924,148	4,166,184,809	6.36	93.64
20 Cents	1,355,000	411,298	943,702	30.35	69.65
Dimes	10,055,455,835	337,500,473	9,717,955,362	3.36	96.64
Three Cents	42,736,240	21,805,398	20,930,842	51.02	48.98
TOTAL	17,328,805,747	1,142,757,674	16,186,048,073	6.59	93.41

More than half the three-cent pieces produced were melted (many of them in 1883); that nearly a third of all 20-cent pieces were likewise melted, and that nearly four in 10 of all silver dollars minted between 1794 and 1935 were melted by the Mint.

Source: Recoinage figures published in Annual Reports of the Director of the Mint, 1883-1950 (67 separate volumes analyzed).

As the stock market has rocketed back and forth over the past two years, the swings in price of the precious metal silver have been far more stable (see chart), and for those playing the Dow Jones Industrial Average, silver has actually surpassed it as a percentage gain. Both, of course, move on a daily basis.

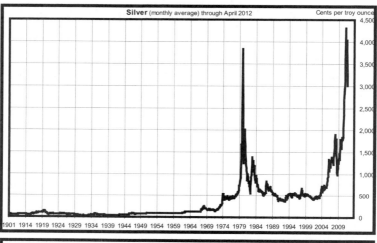

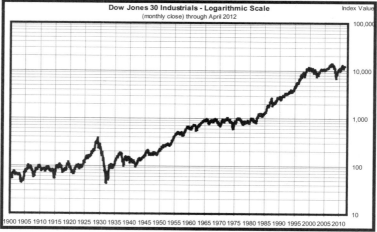

Charts courtesy Commodity Research Bureau.
Silver: Bullion, London (1901-1909); Handy & Harman, New York (1910-1990); Composite (1990-date).

The U.S. Mint has contributed significantly to distribution of silver into the marketplace. Since its silver one-ounce Eagle bullion coin was first issued in 1986, more than 200-million troy ounces of silver have been sold, mostly to investors making purchases of several ounces at a time.

In the last three years, around 70-million ounces of silver have been sold as one-ounce Eagles. Mintage figures of the America the Beautiful silver coins and five-ouncers suggest the numismatic value may well trump silver content—which means that based on mintage, some are definitely undervalued relative to price.

None of this takes into account having big names drop into and out of the silver market. Warren Buffett's announcement some years ago that he had taken a position in silver caused the price of the metal to rise nearly 20 percent before falling back. Then in 1999 Bill Gates announced he was in, too, with 50,000 contracts, which caused silver to jump from $5.35 an ounce to $5.76.

Silver is now more than five times that level, with a very bright and shiny future.

One of the reasons that silver has had such intense activity over the last several years—after a sluggish period in the early 1980s—is that industrial demand has outstripped supply in virtually every year since 1990. Mine production hovers at between 300- to 400-million ounces per year. But a little known fact is that except for the company that Gates bought into, nearly all silver production is done ancillary to other mining, a by-product of mining some other metal that incidentally yields silver.

U.S. and World Silver Production and Price

YEAR	U.S. PRODUCTION (metric tons)	WORLD PRODUCTION (metric tons)	U.S. % of TOTAL	PRICE ($ per troy oz)
1901	1,720	5,380	31.97	0.645
1902	1,730	5,060	34.19	0.569
1903	1,690	5,220	32.38	0.624
1904	1,740	5,110	34.05	0.625
1905	1,750	5,360	32.65	0.665
1906	1,780	5,130	34.70	0.724
1907	1,630	5,730	28.45	0.710
1908	1,580	6,320	25.00	0.589
1909	1,780	6,600	26.97	0.540
1910	1,790	6,900	25.94	0.576
1911	1,900	7,040	26.99	0.570

YEAR	U.S. PRODUCTION (metric tons)	WORLD PRODUCTION (metric tons)	U.S. % of TOTAL	PRICE ($ per troy oz)
1912	2,050	6,980	29.37	0.656
1913	2,210	7,010	31.53	0.651
1914	2,170	5,240	41.41	0.609
1915	2,250	5,730	39.27	0.580
1916	2,450	5,250	46.67	0.790
1917	2,200	5,420	40.59	1.165
1918	2,120	6,140	34.53	1.019
1919	1,610	5,490	29.33	1.383
1920	1,760	5,390	32.65	1.370
1921	1,440	5,330	27.02	0.730
1922	1,900	6,530	29.10	0.740
1923	2,190	7,650	28.63	0.690
1924	1,990	7,450	26.71	0.720
1925	2,070	7,650	27.06	0.730
1926	1,940	7,890	24.59	0.680
1927	1,850	7,900	23.42	0.603
1928	1,800	8,020	22.44	0.639
1929	1,890	8,120	23.28	0.578
1930	1,480	7,740	19.12	0.468
1931	929	6,080	15.28	0.375
1932	712	5,130	13.88	0.310
1933	725	5,340	13.58	0.450
1934	1,030	5,990	17.20	0.550
1935	1,520	6,890	22.06	0.810
1936	1,920	7,920	24.24	0.498
1937	2,240	8,640	25.93	0.468
1938	1,960	8,320	23.56	0.448
1939	2,040	8,300	24.58	0.428
1940	2,230	8,570	26.02	0.356
1941	2,090	8,140	25.68	0.351
1942	1,680	7,780	21.59	0.448
1943	1,290	6,380	20.22	0.448
1944	1,070	5,740	18.64	0.448
1945	903	5,040	17.92	0.705
1946	713	3,970	17.96	0.901
1947	1,110	5,220	21.26	0.863
1948	1,180	5,440	21.69	0.775
1949	1,080	5,570	19.39	0.733
1950	1,320	6,320	20.89	0.800
1951	1,240	6,210	19.97	0.902

YEAR	U.S. PRODUCTION (metric tons)	WORLD PRODUCTION (metric tons)	U.S. % of TOTAL	PRICE ($ per troy oz)
1952	1,230	6,700	18.36	0.880
1953	1,170	6,900	16.96	0.853
1954	1,150	6,670	17.24	0.853
1955	1,160	7,000	16.57	0.920
1956	1,200	7,020	17.09	0.916
1957	1,190	7,190	16.55	0.194
1958	1,060	7,430	14.27	0.904
1959	970	6,910	14.04	0.916
1960	957	7,320	13.07	0.914
1961	1,080	7,370	14.65	1.047
1962	1,140	7,650	14.90	1.220
1963	1,100	7,780	14.14	1.293
1964	1,130	7,730	14.62	1.293
1965	1,240	8,010	15.48	1.293
1966	1,360	8,300	16.39	1.293
1967	1,010	8,030	12.58	2.170
1968	1,020	8,560	11.92	2.560
1969	1,300	9,200	14.13	2.020
1970	1,400	9,360	14.96	1.930
1971	1,290	9,170	14.07	1.750
1972	1,160	9,380	12.37	2.040
1973	1,170	9,700	12.06	3.280
1974	1,050	9,260	11.34	6.700
1975	1,090	9,430	11.56	5.225
1976	1,070	9,840	10.87	5.100
1977	1,190	10,300	11.55	4.960
1978	1,230	10,700	11.50	6.290
1979	1,180	10,800	10.93	28.000
1980	1,010	10,700	9.44	48.000
1981	1,270	11,200	11.34	10.520
1982	1,250	11,500	10.87	7.950
1983	1,350	12,100	11.16	11.440
1984	1,390	13,100	10.61	8.140
1985	1,230	13,100	9.39	6.140
1986	1,070	13,000	8.23	5.440
1987	1,240	14,000	8.86	7.020
1988	1,660	15,500	10.71	6.530
1989	2,010	16,400	12.26	5.490
1990	2,120	16,600	12.77	4.820
1991	1,860	15,600	11.92	4.040

YEAR	U.S. PRODUCTION (metric tons)	WORLD PRODUCTION (metric tons)	U.S. % of TOTAL	PRICE ($ per troy oz)
1992	1,800	14,900	12.08	3.950
1993	1,640	14,100	11.63	4.320
1994	1,490	14,000	10.64	5.310
1995	1,560	14,900	10.47	5.080
1996	1,570	15,100	10.40	5.180
1997	2,180	16,500	13.21	5.945
1998	2,060	17,200	11.98	5.549
1999	1,950	17,600	11.08	5.218
2000	1,980	18,100	10.94	4.951
2001	1,740	18,900	9.21	4.370
2002	1,350	18,800	7.18	4.599
2003	1,240	18,800	6.60	4.876
2004	1,250	19,900	6.28	6.671
2005	1,230	20,600	5.97	7.316
2006	1,140	20,200	5.64	12.050
2007	1,260	20,800	6.06	9.869
2008	1,230	21,300	5.73	14.98
2009	1,230	21,400	5.74	13.37
2010	1,230*	21,600	5.74*	24.50
2011	1,250*	21,800	5.74*	30.00

*estimate

The silver content of any .900 fine quarter ranged between six and 17 cents in the first half of the 20th century. But after silver rose above $1/oz, silver quarters moved above face value. In 1980 at $48/oz, there was $8.63 of silver in quarters. In 2011 at $30/oz, there was $4.43 of silver in quarters.

Data: U.S. Geographical Survey (2012). Metal price quotes (annual) courtesy Kitco. United States production as a percentage of world production calculated by the author.

Supply and demand factors appear poised to keep an upward pressure on prices. Demand has exceeded 500-million ounces every year since 1990, and in several years has gone more than 600-million troy ounces to fuel the industrial economy.

Silver is used for making jewelry, silverware, electronics, batteries, and as a brazing alloy for mirrors.

Photography remains a key element of silver's overall demand. According to the CPM Group, a widely respected industry analyst, there "are no economical substitutes for silver-halide technology." And the higher-quality and faster-speed films that consumers seek, the more silver is required. Digital photography may eventually compete strongly with this, but in recent years, more than 200-million ounces of silver go to the photography sector alone.

Issues concerning photography and industrial use for silver have existed for many years—and are likely to continue into the future.

But silver's price in the future is deeply rooted to its past, when it was a major political issue that was addressed by both the Democratic and Republican political parties and played a dominant role in presidential politics.

Silver's whole modern history has government interference written all over it. When the Coinage Act of 1965 was passed, it had an important clause that ratified the legal tender status of all American coins and currency previously produced (thus, finally legalizing the trade dollar).

In the hearing held June 4, 1965, Rep. Wright Patman, the powerful chair of the House Banking & Currency Committee, asked Treasury Secretary Henry Fowler whether the coins being authorized "will have the stamp of the United

President Lincoln visits General McClellan and his staff at Antietam, MD, battlefield on October 3, 1862.

By way of example, an advertiser in the New York *Commercial Times* on July 10, 1863 reported that gold coin was at a 17 percent premium to paper currency, silver at 10 percent, and nickel at four percent. In *History of the Greenbacks* (1903), 100 one-cent (copper) coins had a value of 55-cents in gold; in July, 1862, the paper value of dollars was 86.6 cents in gold, and the metal in 100 nickel cents was quoted at 63.5 cents in paper.

In 2012, we simply accept that all coins and paper money are equal—because in our common experience, the legal tender laws have made them so. We are so far removed from the monetary bedlam of the 19th century that it's important to keep in mind if we fail to take the proper precautions, it could happen again.

States recognizing that each coin is legal tender for all debts, public and private," to which Fowler replied in the affirmative.

On pages 20 to 21 of the hearing, Fowler was asked, "If they [business entities] have something owed to them, they are compelled by law to accept these coins," to which Fowler answered, "Correct." Chairman Patman clarified "two points on the record" on page 32 of the same hearing:

"All coins, all paper money are of equal value as legal tender. You can pay a million dollar debt with copper cents if you want to. That has not always been true. You can pay any debt with five-cent pieces or 25-cent pieces, and it makes no difference. It is all acceptable legal tender." Secretary Fowler then acknowledged that some vending machines don't accept half dollars and that some coin-operated vending machines are limited. On the floor debates, it was further clarified that this was nothing more than a "restatement of existing law."

Congress and the drafters of the Coinage Act of 1965 knew their history. Wright Patman, the old populist, certainly did—"of how there were different rates and values for different coins;" how quoted prices for gold coin, silver coin, federal currency and local paper money varied—exactly what the officials at this hearing desperately wanted to avoid.

SILVER COINS REMAIN a good way to acquire silver metal. They can be bought for their numismatic content, their silver weight or their rarity. Though the Mint and Congress intended the five-ounce silver coin to be a purely bullion item, the modest mintages suggest this "bullion" item will become numismatic very quickly.

Silver was and remains an alluring metal. It caught the political climate of the 19th century at the right time. When William Jennings Bryan, the Democratic nominee for president in 1900 gave his "Cross of Gold" speech, he was arguing for an expanded role of gold and silver coin in the monetary system.

Jennings Bryan said, "Having behind us the producing masses of this nation and the world, supported by the commercial interests, the laboring interests and the toilers everywhere, we will answer their demand for a gold standard by saying to them: You shall not press down upon the brow of labor this crown of thorns, you shall not crucify mankind upon a cross of gold."

Chapter Eight
The Legislation

THERE ARE TWO KEY legislative components to the America the Beautiful National Parks Coin Program: the House Report (from the committee on Financial Services), and Public Law 110–456, approved December 23, 2008, also found in 122 Stat 5038. (The abbreviated "legal" looking terms means that it was the 456th law enacted in the 110th Congress.)

The House Report

JULY 8, 2008- Committed to the Committee of the Whole House on the State of the Union and ordered to be printed

Mr. FRANK of Massachusetts, from the Committee on Financial Services, submitted the following

REPORT
[To accompany H.R. 6184]

[Including cost estimate of the Congressional Budget Office]

The Committee on Financial Services, to whom was referred the bill (H.R. 6184) to provide for a program for circulating quarter-dollar coins that are emblematic of a national park or other national site in each State, the District of Columbia, and each territory of the United States, and for other purposes, having considered the same, report favorably thereon without amendment and recommend that the bill do pass.

CONTENTS Page
Purpose and Summary
Background and Need for Legislation
Hearings
Committee Consideration

Committee Votes
Committee Oversight Findings
Performance Goals and Objectives
   New Budget Authority, Entitlement Authority, and Tax
Expenditures
Committee Cost Estimate
Congressional Budget Office Estimate
Federal Mandates Statement
Advisory Committee Statement
Constitutional Authority Statement
Applicability to Legislative Branch
Earmark Identification
Section-by-Section Analysis of the Legislation
Changes in Existing Law Made by the Bill, as Reported

PURPOSE AND SUMMARY

The "America's Beautiful National Parks Quarter Dollar Coin Act of 2008" intends to create a beautiful, educational and logical successor to the 50-State quarter program that ends in 2008, and to its one-year successor program that honors the District of Columbia and the five territories on the reverse of the quarter in 2009. Beginning in 2009, quarters issued would bear designs honoring one national park in each of the 50 States plus the District of Columbia and the territories, with five designs issued a year in the order the sites were designated as national sites. In addition, a unique investment-grade silver bullion coin would be available for sale through the normal investor network but also available for bulk purchase by a designee of the National Park Service so that the investment coins could be sold as mementos at various national sites including those chosen to be represented on circulating quarter dollars. The investment grade coins would be three-inches in diameter, contain five-ounces of .999 fine silver and bear exact replicas of the quarter-dollar designs, issued only in the year when the comparable circulating quarter was issued.

BACKGROUND AND NEED FOR LEGISLATION

H.R. 6184 was introduced June 4, 2008, by Mr. Castle, for himself, Mrs. Maloney and Mr. Gutierrez. The bill seeks to build on the success of the widely popular 50-State quarter program, which will end this year, followed by a one-year program during which the United States Mint will issue quarter-dollars with reverses honoring the District of Columbia and the five territories.

H.R. 6184 would replace the images representing the various states on the reverse of the quarter with images of America's national parks. Taking the structure of the State quarter program, it calls for five different designs a year, with the coins issued in the order in which the national park was designated either by the President or by Congress. All 50 states, plus the District of Columbia and the territories, would be honored, and after the first round of 56 quarters the Treasury Secretary could opt to do a second 56 coins, honoring a second national site in each state or territory.

To allow the proper ordering of the 56 designs, the legislation requires the Treasury Secretary, in consultation with the Secretary of the Interior, the chief executive of each state or territory, and other appropriate federal officials, to choose the complete list within 270 days of enactment. It allows for the selection of a national site other than a national park in the event that a national seashore, or a national monument or similar site is more significant to a particular state and its residents, and to the country, than a national park in that state. Coin reverse designs would be chosen by the Treasury Secretary in a manner similar to the method for choosing the State quarter designs. At the end of the program— after either the first 56 or a second 56 coins—the reverse design would become a depiction of General Washington crossing the Delaware River prior to the Battle of Trenton.

Michael Castle, R-DE (b. 1939), is the legislative father of the "America the Beautiful" circulating commemorative coin program. Educated at Hamilton College, he received his law degree from Georgetown University in 1964. He was Delaware's governor from 1985 to 1992 and was elected to Congress in 1993. After an unsuccessful bid for U.S. Senate in 2010, he retired from the House in 2011. The expansion of the State Quarters Program to National Parks is something he remains proud of.

Additionally, the bill creates an unusual investment-grade silver coin that would be three-inches in diameter and be made of five-ounces of .999 fine silver, and be issued bearing exact duplicates of the quarters. The bullion, investment-grade coins would be issued and for sale only during the year in which the equivalent quarter design is issued. The coins are expected to have appeal to investors as a hedge against inflation, and be available for sale through the normal investment-coin network, but the bill also makes special arrangements for the National Park Service or its designee to buy the bullion coins in bulk and make them available for sale at the national parks or other national sites represented on the quarters as mementos.

HEARINGS
No hearings were held on H.R. 6184 in the 110th Congress.

COMMITTEE CONSIDERATION
The Committee on Financial Services met in open session on June 24, 2008, and ordered reported H.R. 6184, America's Beautiful National Parks Quarter Dollar Coin Act of 2008, to the House with a favorable recommendation by a record vote of 58 yeas and 0 nays.

COMMITTEE VOTES
Clause 3(b) of rule XIII of the Rules of the House of Representatives requires the committee to list the record votes on the motion to report legislation and amendments thereto. A motion by Mr. Frank to report the bill to the House with a favorable recommendation was agreed to by a record vote of 58 yeas and 0 nays (Record vote no. FC-111). * * *

COMMITTEE OVERSIGHT FINDINGS
Pursuant to clause 3(c)(1) of rule XIII of the Rules of the House of Representatives, the Committee has held hearings and made findings that are reflected in this report.

PERFORMANCE GOALS AND OBJECTIVES
Pursuant to clause 3(c)(4) of rule XIII of the Rules of the House of Representatives, the committee establishes the following performance related goals and objectives for this legislation:

The U.S. Mint will have succeeded at the rollout of this program if it has selected the 56 sites to be depicted on the first round of `National Park' quarters after having worked closely with the Interior Secretary, other federal officials and the chief executives of the states and territories, in time to design the first five designs and put together a marketing program in time to issue the first of the new series of quarter dollars in January 2010. Additionally, success will be evidenced by having developed a source of supply for the unique bullion coins, and a marketing program for them, so that they may be issued beginning in 2010 as well.

NEW BUDGET AUTHORITY, ENTITLEMENT AUTHORITY, AND TAX EXPENDITURES
In compliance with clause 3(c)(2) of rule XIII of the Rules of the House of Representatives, the committee adopts as its own the estimate of new budget authority, entitlement authority, or tax expenditures or revenues contained in the cost estimate prepared by the Director of the Congressional Budget Office pursuant to section 402 of the Congressional Budget Act of 1974.

COMMITTEE COST ESTIMATE

The committee adopts as its own the cost estimate prepared by the Director of the Congressional Budget Office pursuant to section 402 of the Congressional Budget Act of 1974.

CONGRESSIONAL BUDGET OFFICE ESTIMATE

Pursuant to clause 3(c)(3) of rule XIII of the Rules of the House of Representatives, the following is the cost estimate provided by the Congressional Budget Office pursuant to section 402 of the Congressional Budget Act of 1974:

July 8, 2008.
Hon. Barney Frank,
Chairman, Committee on Financial Services,
House of Representatives, Washington, D.C.

Dear Mr. Chairman: The Congressional Budget Office has prepared the enclosed cost estimate for H.R. 6184, the America's Beautiful National Parks Quarter Dollar Coin Act of 2008.

If you wish further details on this estimate, we will be pleased to provide them. The CBO staff contact is Matthew Pickford.

Sincerely,

Peter R. Orszag.

Enclosure.

H.R. 6184—America's Beautiful National Parks Quarter Dollar Coin Act of 2008

Summary: H.R. 6184 would authorize the U.S. Mint to make changes to the design of the quarter-dollar coin to feature one national park or other national site in each state, the District of Columbia, and each territory beginning in 2010. In addition, the legislation would require production of a new silver bullion coin bearing the same design as the quarter dollar.

CBO estimates that enacting this bill would reduce direct spending by $26 million over the 2010-2018 period. H.R. 6184 contains no intergovernmental or private-sector mandates as defined in the Unfunded Mandates Reform Act (UMRA) and would not affect the budgets of state, local, or tribal governments. * * *

In addition to the budgetary effects summarized in the table, by increasing the public's holding of coins, H.R. 6184 also would provide the government with additional resources for financing the federal deficit. The seigniorage (or profit) from placing the additional coins in circulation—the difference between the face value of the coins and the cost of production—would reduce the amount the government needs to borrow from the public. CBO estimates that seigniorage resulting from the bill would amount to about $785 million over the 2010-2018 period. Under the principles established by the President's 1967 Commission on Budget Concepts, seigniorage does not directly affect the budget, but is treated as a means of financing the deficit.

Basis of estimate: H.R. 6184 would direct the Secretary of the Treasury to design and issue a series of quarters that feature one national park or other national site in each state, the District of Columbia, and each territory (for a total of 56) over an 11-year period, beginning in 2010. During this period, designs for each national park or other national site in each state would replace the eagle design on the reverse side of the George Washington quarter that is scheduled to be used again in 2010 following the end of the state quarters series.

The Mint would issue five quarters a year in the order that the national sites were established. The Secretary of the Treasury would select the sites within 270 days of enactment in consultation with the Secretary of the Interior, the governor or other chief executive of each state, territory, or the District of Columbia. The design selection would be made by the Secretary of the Treasury after consultation with the Secretary of the Interior and the Commission on Fine Arts. The Citizens Coinage Advisory Committee would review the designs. After the new National Parks Quarter Dollar Program ends, the quarter-dollar reverse design would contain an image of Washington crossing the Delaware prior to the Battle of Trenton.

The bill also would direct the Mint to produce a silver bullion coin bearing the same designs as the circulating quarter dollars that would only be available during the calendar year the circulating coin is issued. The 0.999 fine silver bullion coins would have a diameter of three-inches and weigh five-ounces. The distribution of the bullion coins would be made through authorized dealers or through the National Park Service or a designee.

NATIONAL PARKS QUARTER DOLLAR PROGRAM
Beginning in 2010, H.R. 6184 would authorize the Mint to sell

uncirculated and proof coins, both made of copper-nickel and silver. CBO expects that the Mint would sell a variety of proof and silver sets of the redesigned quarter dollar. Since those are commercial products, the receipts would constitute offsetting collections to the Mint. Based on information from the Mint and historical sales and profit information for the 50 State Quarters Program, CBO estimates that those sales would increase offsetting collections to the Mint by about $30 million annually, for a total of about $263 million over the 2010-2018 period. Based on the cost of previous Mint sets, CBO estimates that the Mint would retain and spend about $27 million annually of the increased offsetting collections to cover the costs of producing the coins, at a total cost of about $237 million over the 2010-2018 period. The Mint must transfer any excess funds it generates from sales to the general fund of the Treasury. CBO estimates that net receipts to the Treasury, therefore, would total about $3 million annually or $26 million over the 2010-2018 period.

Rep. Barney Frank, D-MA (b. 1940), who chaired the House Financial Services Committee during the legislative consideration of the "America the Beautiful" quarter creation process, leaves Congress at the end of 2012 with a list of solid numismatic legislative accomplishments.

He managed to achieve a rare consensus by pointing out the profit potential from circulating commemorative coinage. Frank went to Bayonne High School in New Jersey before graduating from Harvard and Harvard Law School.

SILVER BULLION COIN

H.R. 6184 would direct the Mint to produce a quarter-dollar coin of 0.999 fine silver bullion for investors. The new silver bullion coin would be produced in the same sequence as the coins in the National Parks Quarter Dollar Program. Based on information from the Mint and the numismatic and investment community, CBO expects that sales of the silver bullion coins would be small. Thus, we estimate that the silver bullion coins would generate less than $500,000 a year in excess of production costs; that amount would be recorded in the budget as offsetting receipts.

SEIGNIORAGE

In addition to the bill's effects on direct spending, by increasing the public's holding of quarters, H.R. 6184 also would result in the government's acquiring additional resources for financing the federal deficit in the form of seigniorage—the difference between the face value of coins and the cost to produce them. The Mint's 50

State Quarters Program has been credited with generating renewed interest in holding more coins by collectors and the public. The production of quarters increased from about 1.5 billion over the 1989-1998 period to over six billion in fiscal year 2000 when the 50 State Quarters Program began. By fiscal year 2007, however, demand for quarters had fallen to about 2.7 billion quarters. The Mint estimates that the 50 State Quarters Program has generated about $3.5 billion of seigniorage since the program began in 1999.

CBO expects that enacting the bill would lead to a greater production of quarters, although not as many as the 50 State Quarters Program. The seigniorage, or profit, from placing the additional coins in circulation would reduce the amount of government borrowing from the public. Quarter-dollar production has averaged about 3.5-billion coins a year over the past nine years, and the seigniorage is about 15.2-cents per coin. However, over the past five years, quarter-dollar production has diminished to about 2.6-billion coins a year. Based on information from the Mint and the numismatic community, CBO expects that quarter-dollar production under the National Parks Quarter Dollar Program would be about two-billion coins annually, or almost 600 million more quarter-dollar coins a year than would otherwise be produced. CBO estimates that seigniorage earned by the federal government would increase by about $785 million over the 10-year period.

Intergovernmental and private-sector impact: H.R. 6184 contains no intergovernmental or private-sector mandates as defined in UMRA, and would not affect the budgets of state, local, or tribal governments.

Estimate prepared by: Federal Costs: Matthew Pickford; Impact on State, Local, and Tribal Governments: Elizabeth Cove; Impact on the Private Sector: Paige Piper/Bach.

Estimate approved by: Peter H. Fontaine, Assistant Director for Budget Analysis.

FEDERAL MANDATES STATEMENT
The committee adopts as its own the estimate of federal mandates prepared by the Director of the Congressional Budget Office pursuant to section 423 of the Unfunded Mandates Reform Act.

ADVISORY COMMITTEE STATEMENT
No advisory committees within the meaning of section 5(b) of the Federal Advisory Committee Act were created by this legislation.

CONSTITUTIONAL AUTHORITY STATEMENT

Pursuant to clause 3(d)(1) of rule XIII of the Rules of the House of Representatives, the committee finds that the Constitutional Authority of Congress to enact this legislation is provided by Article 1, section 8, clause 1 (relating to the general welfare of the United States) and clause 3 (relating to the power to regulate interstate commerce).

APPLICABILITY TO LEGISLATIVE BRANCH

The committee finds that the legislation does not relate to the terms and conditions of employment or access to public services or accommodations within the meaning of section 102(b)(3) of the Congressional Accountability Act.

EARMARK IDENTIFICATION

H.R. 6184 does not contain any congressional earmarks, limited tax benefits, or limited tariff benefits as defined in clause 9 of rule XXI.

SECTION-BY-SECTION ANALYSIS OF H.R. 6184
Section 1. Short title

This section establishes the short title of the bill, the "America's Beautiful National Parks Quarter Dollar Coin Act of 2008".

TITLE I—NATIONAL SITE QUARTER DOLLARS
Section 101—Findings

Congress finds that: Yellowstone National Park became the nation's first national park in 1872; President Theodore Roosevelt is considered by many to be our `Conservationist President'; that the National Park System now includes 391 areas and about 84-million acres; and numerous other types of national sites have been placed under various forms of conservancy, such as the national forests and sites within the National Wildlife Refuge System and on the National Register of Historic Places.

Section 102—Issuance of quarter-dollars emblematic of national parks or other national sites, in each state, the District of Columbia and each territory

It was directed that beginning in 2010, quarter-dollars shall have designs on the reverse depicting one national site in each of the states, and in the District of Columbia and the territories. Five designs are to be issued each year in the order that the sites were recognized as national sites, determined after the Treasury Secretary working with the Interior Secretary (or other appropriate Federal officials and state governors), selects one site per state. National sites are defined as including national parks as well as any other nationally recognized site such as a national wildlife refuge. Allows for the issue of the coins in various numismatic forms, including solid-silver versions, and allows for a complete second round of the quarters recognizing a second national site in each state, after proper notice to the committees of jurisdiction. Designs would be selected by the Treasury Secretary after appropriate consultations. Provides that the design on the reverse of the coin after the national parks quarter program is concluded will be a representation of General George Washington crossing the Delaware River before the Battle of Trenton.

Theodore Roosevelt (1858-1919), a noted conservationist as well as president (1901-1909), had an impact on the national park system extending well beyond his term in office. The same is true of his numismatic legacy.

TR signed legislation establishing five national parks: Crater Lake, Oregon; Wind Cave, South Dakota; Sullys Hill, North Dakota (later redesignated a game preserve); Mesa Verde, Colorado; and Platt, Oklahoma (now part of Chickasaw National Recreation Area).

The Antiquities Act of June 8, 1906 enabled Roosevelt and his successors to proclaim "historic landmarks, historic or prehistoric structures, and other objects of historic or scientific interest" in federal ownership as national monuments. Later presidents used the Antiquities Act to proclaim national monuments. Forty-nine of them retain this designation today.

TITLE II—BULLION INVESTMENT PRODUCT

Section 201—Silver bullion coin

Provides for the minting and issuing of investment-grade, silver-bullion coins that are three-inches in diameter and made of five-ounces of .999 fine silver. Such coins shall be exact duplicates of the quarter-dollars and carry that denomination, and would be sold through the Mint's regular authorized dealer network for investment products. They would also be made available for bulk purchase by the representative of the National Park Service Director, so that they may be sold as a memento at various national sites including those honored by the actual quarter-dollar coin reverse designs. The investment-grade coins could not be minted as so-called 'fractional' coins and would only be available for purchase during the year in which the corresponding quarter-dollar reverse design was available.

CHANGES IN EXISTING LAW MADE BY THE BILL, AS REPORTED

In compliance with clause 3(e) of rule XIII of the Rules of the House of Representatives, changes in existing law made by the bill, as reported, are shown as follows (new matter is printed in italic and existing law in which no change is proposed is shown in roman):

TITLE 31, UNITED STATES CODE
* * * * * * *

Subtitle IV--MONEY
* * * * * * *

CHAPTER 51—COINS AND CURRENCY
* * * * * * *

SUBCHAPTER II—GENERAL AUTHORITY
* * * * * * *

Sec. 5112. Denominations, specifications, and design of coins

(t) Redesign and Issuance of Quarter Dollars Emblematic of National Sites in Each State, the District of Columbia, and Each Territory—

(1) REDESIGN BEGINNING UPON COMPLETION OF PRIOR PROGRAM-

(A) IN GENERAL- Notwithstanding the fourth sentence of subsection (d)(1) and subsection (d)(2), quarter-dollars issued beginning in 2010 shall have designs on the reverse selected in accordance with this subsection, which are emblematic of the national sites in the states, the District of Columbia and the territories of the United States.

(B) FLEXIBILITY WITH REGARD TO PLACEMENT OF INSCRIPTIONS- Notwithstanding subsection (d)(1), the Secretary may select a design for quarter-dollars referred to in subparagraph (A) in which—

(i) the inscription described in the second sentence of subsection (d)(1) appears on the reverse side of any such quarter-dollars; and

(ii) any inscription described in the third sentence of subsection (d)(1) or the designation of the value of the coin appears on the obverse side of any such quarter-dollars.

(C) INCLUSION OF DISTRICT OF COLUMBIA, AND TERRITORIES- For purposes of this subsection, the term 'State' has the same meaning as in section 3(a)(3) of the Federal Deposit Insurance Act.

(2) SINGLE SITE IN EACH STATE- The design on the reverse side of each quarter-dollar issued during the period of issuance under this subsection shall be emblematic of one national site in each state.

(3) SELECTION OF SITE AND DESIGN-

(A) SITE-

(i) IN GENERAL-

(ii) TIMING- The selection process under clause (i) shall be completed before the end of the 270-day period beginning on the date of the enactment of the America's Beautiful National Parks Quarter Dollar Coin Act of 2008.

(B) DESIGN- Each of the designs required under this subsection for quarter-dollars shall be—

(i) selected by the Secretary after consultation with—

(I) the Secretary of the Interior; and

(II) the Commission of Fine Arts; and

(ii) reviewed by the Citizens Coinage Advisory Committee.

(C) SELECTION AND APPROVAL PROCESS- Recommendations for site selections and designs for quarter dollars may be submitted in accordance with the site and design selection and approval process developed by the Secretary in the sole discretion of the Secretary.

(D) PARTICIPATION IN DESIGN- The Secretary may include participation by officials of the State, artists from the State, engravers of the U. S. Mint, and members of the general public.

(E) STANDARDS- Because it is important that the nation's coinage and currency bear dignified designs of which the citizens of the United States can be proud, the Secretary shall not select any frivolous or inappropriate design for any quarter-dollar minted under this subsection.

(F) PROHIBITION ON CERTAIN REPRESENTATIONS- No head and shoulders portrait or bust of any person, living or dead, no portrait of a living person, and no outline or map of a state may be included in the design on the reverse of any quarter-dollar under this subsection.

(4) ISSUANCE OF COINS-

(A) ORDER OF ISSUANCE- The quarter-dollar coins issued under this subsection bearing designs of national sites shall be issued in the order in which the sites selected under paragraph (3) were first established as a national site.

(B) RATE OF ISSUANCE- The quarter-dollar coins bearing designs of national sites under this subsection shall be issued at the rate of five new designs during each year of the period of issuance under this subsection.

U.S. Mint engraver and sculptor Don Everhart II (b. 1949) designed (but ultimately did not sculpt) the first of the America the Beautiful national park coins. His distinctive style first found success at the Franklin Mint, and since 2004 he has been at the Philadelphia Mint, leading the charge to revitalize American coinage.

Since joining the U.S. Mint staff, Everhart has designed or sculpted more than 35 U.S. coins and 16 Congressionally authorized national medals. His private commissions include the popular "Dinosaur" series for collectors, and his work is represented in the permanent collections of the Smithsonian, the British Museum, National Sculpture Society and the American Numismatic Society.

(C) NUMBER OF EACH OF FIVE COIN DESIGNS IN EACH YEAR- Of the quarter dollar coins issued during each year of the period of issuance, the Secretary of the Treasury shall prescribe, on the basis of such factors as the Secretary determines to be appropriate, the number of quarter-dollars which shall be issued with each of the designs selected for such year.

(5) TREATMENT AS NUMISMATIC ITEMS- For purposes of sections 5134 and 5136, all coins minted under this subsection shall be considered to be numismatic items.

(6) ISSUANCE-

(A) QUALITY OF COINS- The Secretary may mint and issue such number of quarter-dollars of each design selected under paragraph (3) in uncirculated and proof qualities as the Secretary determines to be appropriate.

(B) SILVER COINS- Notwithstanding subsection (b), the Secretary may mint and issue such number of quarter dollars of each design selected under paragraph (3) as the Secretary determines to be appropriate, with a content of 90-percent silver and 10-percent copper.

(7) PERIOD OF ISSUANCE-

(A) IN GENERAL- Subject to paragraph (2), the program established under this subsection shall continue in effect until a national site in each State has been honored.

(B) SECOND ROUND AT DISCRETION OF SECRETARY-

(i) DETERMINATION- The Secretary may make a determination before the end of the nine-year period beginning when the first quarter-dollar is issued under this subsection to continue the period of issuance until a second national site in each state, the District of Columbia, and each territory referred to in this subsection has been honored with a design on a quarter-dollar.

(ii) NOTICE AND REPORT- Within 30 days after making a determination under clause (i), the Secretary shall submit a written report on such determination to the committee on Financial Services of the House of Representatives and the committee on Banking, Housing, and Urban Affairs of the Senate.

(iii) APPLICABILITY OF PROVISIONS- If the Secretary makes a determination under clause (i), the provisions of this subsection applicable to site and design selection and approval, the order, timing, and conditions of issuance shall apply in like manner as the initial issuance of quarter-dollars under this subsection, except that the issuance of quarter-dollars pursuant to such determination bearing the first design shall commence in order immediately following the last issuance of quarter-dollars under the first round.

(iv) CONTINUATION UNTIL ALL STATES ARE HONORED- If the Secretary makes a determination under clause (i), the program under this subsection shall continue until a second site in each State has been so honored.

Henrietta Fore and David L. Ganz, 2001

DESIGNS AFTER END OF PROGRAM- Upon the completion of the coin program under this subsection, the design on—

(A) the obverse of the quarter-dollar shall revert to the same design containing an image of President Washington in effect for the quarter-dollar before the institution of the 50-State quarter-dollar program; and

(B) notwithstanding the fourth sentence of subsection (d)(1), the reverse of the quarter-dollar shall contain an image of General Washington crossing the Delaware River prior to the Battle of Trenton.

Henrietta Holsman Fore (b. 1948), appointed by President George W. Bush as 37th director of the Mint (2001-2005), was one of the most innovative directors of the past hundred years. She introduced "artistic fusion" into the Mint's vocabulary and fundamentally changed the artistic approach to circulating coin design.

More than 20 major bills affecting coinage and metal were initiated on her watch, including multiple designs for the Lincoln cent during his centennial and birth year.

(9) NATIONAL SITE- For purposes of this subsection, the term 'national site' means any site under the supervision, management, or conservancy of the National Park Service, the United States Forest Service, the United States Fish and Wildlife Service, or any similar department or agency of the Federal

Government, including any national park, national monument, national battlefield, national military park, national historical park, national historic site, national lakeshore, seashore, recreation area, parkway, scenic river, or trail and any site in the National Wildlife Refuge System.

(10) APPLICATION IN EVENT OF INDEPENDENCE- If any territory becomes independent or otherwise ceases to be a territory or possession of the United States before quarter-dollars bearing designs which are emblematic of such territory are minted pursuant to this subsection, this subsection shall cease to apply with respect to such territory.

Henry S. Reuss (1912-2002) served in the House of Representatives for 28 years. On his watch, Americans regained the right to privately own gold, and America's bicentennial was marked with three circulating commemorative coins.

Born in Milwaukee, Reuss studied at Cornell and Harvard Law School. It was his progressive leadership that set the stage for the revival of commemorative coinage starting in 1982, without which the America the Beautiful Program would not exist.

(u) Silver Bullion Investment Product-

(1) IN GENERAL- The Secretary shall strike and make available for sale such number of bullion coins as the Secretary determines to be appropriate that are exact duplicates of the quarter-dollars issued under subsection (t), each of which shall—

(A) have a diameter of 3.0 inches and weigh 5.0 ounces;

(B) contain .999 fine silver;

(C) have incused into the edge the fineness and weight of the bullion coin;

(D) bear an inscription of the denomination of such coin, which shall be 'quarter dollar'; and

(E) not be minted or issued by the U.S. Mint as so-called 'fractional' bullion coins or in any size other than the size described in paragraph (A).

(2) AVAILABILITY FOR SALE- Bullion coins minted under paragraph (1)—

(A) shall become available for sale no sooner than the first day of the calendar year in which the circulating quarter-dollar of which such bullion coin is a duplicate is issued; and

(B) may only be available for sale during the year in which such circulating quarter-dollar is issued.

(3) DISTRIBUTION-

(A) IN GENERAL- In addition to the authorized dealers utilized by the Secretary in distributing bullion coins and solely for purposes of distributing bullion coins issued under this subsection, the Director of the National Park Service, or the designee of the Director, may purchase numismatic items issued under this subsection, but only in units of no fewer than 1,000 at a time, and the Director, or the Director's designee, may resell or repackage such numismatic items as the Director determines to be appropriate.

(B) RESALE- The Director of the National Park Service, or the designee of the Director, may resell, at cost and without repackaging, numismatic items acquired by the Director or such designee under subparagraph (A) to any party affiliated with any national site honored by a quarter dollar under subsection (t) for repackaging and resale by such party in the same manner and to the same extent as such party would be authorized to engage in such activities under subparagraph (A) if the party were acting as the designee of the Director under such subparagraph.

H.R. 6184

One Hundred Tenth Congress

of the

United States of America

AT THE SECOND SESSION

Begun and held at the City of Washington on Thursday,
the third day of January, two thousand and eight

An Act

To provide for a program for circulating quarter dollar coins that are
emblematic of a national park or other national site in each State,
the District of Columbia, and each territory of the United States, and
for other purposes.

*Be it enacted by the Senate and House of Representatives of the
United States of America in Congress assembled,*

SECTION 1. SHORT TITLE.

This Act may be cited as the 'America's Beautiful National Parks
Quarter Dollar Coin Act of 2008'.

TITLE I--NATIONAL SITE QUARTER DOLLARS

SEC. 101. FINDINGS.

The Congress finds as follows:

(1) Yellowstone National Park was established by an Act signed by President Ulysses S. Grant on March 1, 1872, as the Nation's first national park.

(2) The summer and autumn of 1890 saw the establishment of a number of national sites:

(A) August 19: Chickamauga and Chattanooga established as national military parks in Georgia and Tennessee.

(B) August 30: Antietam established as a national battlefield site in Maryland.

(C) September 25: Sequoia National Park established in California.

(D) September 27: Rock Creek Park established in the District of Columbia.

(E) October 1: General Grant National Park established in California (and subsequently incorporated in Kings Canyon National Park).

(F) October 1: Yosemite National Park established in California.

(3) Theodore Roosevelt was this nation's 26th President and is considered by many to be our 'Conservationist President'.

(4) As a frequent visitor to the West, Theodore Roosevelt witnessed the virtual destruction of some big game species and the overgrazing that destroyed the grasslands and with them the habitats for small mammals and songbirds and conservation increasingly became one of his major concerns.

(5) When he became President in 1901, Roosevelt pursued this interest in conservation by establishing the first 51 Bird Reserves, 4 Game Preserves, and 150 National Forests.

(6) He also established the United States Forest Service, signed

into law the creation of 5 National Parks, and signed the Act for the Preservation of American Antiquities in 1906 under which he proclaimed 18 national monuments.

(7) Approximately 230,000,000 acres of area within the United States was placed under public protection by Theodore Roosevelt.

(8) Theodore Roosevelt said that nothing short of defending this country in wartime 'compares in importance with the great central task of leaving this land even a better land for our descendants than it is for us'.

(9) The National Park Service was created by an Act signed by President Woodrow Wilson on August 25, 1916.

(10) The National Park System comprises 391 areas covering more than 84,000,000 acres in every State (except Delaware), the District of Columbia, American Samoa, Guam, Puerto Rico, and the Virgin Islands.

(11) The sites or areas within the National Park System vary widely in size and type from vast natural wilderness to birthplaces of Presidents to world heritage archaeology sites to an African burial ground memorial in Manhattan and include national parks, monuments, battlefields, military parks, historical parks, historic sites, lakeshores, seashores, recreation areas, scenic rivers and trails, and the White House.

(12) In addition to the sites within the National Park System, the United States has placed numerous other types of sites under various forms of conservancy, such as the national forests and sites within the National Wildlife Refuge System and on the National Register of Historic Places.

SEC. 102. ISSUANCE OF REDESIGNED QUARTER DOLLARS EMBLEMATIC OF NATIONAL PARKS OR OTHER NATIONAL SITES IN EACH STATE, THE DISTRICT OF COLUMBIA, AND EACH TERRITORY.

Section 5112 of title 31, United States Code, is amended by adding at the end the following new subsection:

'(t) Redesign and Issuance of Quarter Dollars Emblematic of National Sites in Each State, the District of Columbia, and Each Territory-

'(1) REDESIGN BEGINNING UPON COMPLETION OF PRIOR PROGRAM-

'(A) IN GENERAL- Notwithstanding the fourth sentence of subsection (d)(1) and subsection (d)(2), quarter dollars issued beginning in 2010 shall have designs on the reverse selected in accordance with this subsection which are emblematic of the national sites in the States, the District of Columbia and the territories of the United States.

'(B) FLEXIBILITY WITH REGARD TO PLACEMENT OF INSCRIPTIONS- Notwithstanding subsection (d)(1), the Secretary may select a design for quarter dollars referred to in subparagraph (A) in which--

'(i) the inscription described in the second sentence of subsection (d)(1) appears on the reverse side of any such quarter dollars; and

'(ii) any inscription described in the third sentence of subsection (d)(1) or the designation of the value of the coin appears on the obverse side of any such quarter dollars.

'(C) INCLUSION OF DISTRICT OF COLUMBIA, AND TERRITORIES- For purposes of this subsection, the term 'State' has the same meaning as in section 3(a)(3) of the Federal Deposit Insurance Act.

'(2) SINGLE SITE IN EACH STATE- The design on the reverse side of each quarter dollar issued during the period of issuance under this subsection shall be emblematic of 1 national site in each State.

'(3) SELECTION OF SITE AND DESIGN-

'(A) SITE-

'(i) IN GENERAL- The selection of a national park or other national site in each State to be honored with a coin under this subsection shall be made by the Secretary of the Treasury, after consultation with the Secretary of the Interior and the governor or other chief executive of each State with respect to which a coin is to be issued under this subsection, and after giving full and thoughtful consideration to national sites that are not under the jurisdiction of the Secretary of the Interior so that the national site chosen for each State shall be the most appropriate in terms of natural or historic significance.

'(ii) TIMING- The selection process under clause (i) shall be completed before the end of the 270-day period beginning on the date of the enactment of the America's Beautiful National Parks Quarter Dollar Coin Act of 2008.

'(B) DESIGN- Each of the designs required under this subsection for quarter dollars shall be--

'(i) selected by the Secretary after consultation with--

'(I) the Secretary of the Interior; and

'(II) the Commission of Fine Arts; and

'(ii) reviewed by the Citizens Coinage Advisory Committee.

'(C) SELECTION AND APPROVAL PROCESS- Recommendations for site selections and designs for quarter dollars may be submitted in accordance with the site and design selection and approval process developed by the Secretary in the sole discretion of the Secretary.

'(D) PARTICIPATION IN DESIGN- The Secretary may include participation by officials of the State, artists from the State, engravers of the United States Mint, and members of the general public.

'(E) STANDARDS- Because it is important that the Nation's coinage and currency bear dignified designs of which the citizens of the United States can be proud, the Secretary shall not select any frivolous or inappropriate design for any quarter dollar minted under this subsection.

'(F) PROHIBITION ON CERTAIN REPRESENTATIONS- No head and shoulders portrait or bust of any person, living or dead, no portrait of a living person, and no outline or map of a State may be included in the design on the reverse of any quarter dollar under this subsection.

'(4) ISSUANCE OF COINS-

'(A) ORDER OF ISSUANCE- The quarter dollar coins issued under this subsection bearing designs of national sites shall be issued in the order in which the sites selected under paragraph (3) were first established as a national site.

'(B) RATE OF ISSUANCE- The quarter dollar coins bearing designs of national sites under this subsection shall be issued at the rate of 5 new designs during each year of the period of issuance under this subsection.

'(C) NUMBER OF EACH OF 5 COIN DESIGNS IN EACH YEAR- Of the quarter dollar coins issued during each year of the period of issuance, the Secretary of the Treasury shall prescribe, on the basis of such factors as the Secretary determines to be appropriate, the number of quarter dollars which shall be issued with each of the designs selected for such year.

'(5) TREATMENT AS NUMISMATIC ITEMS- For purposes of sections 5134 and 5136, all coins minted under this subsection shall be considered to be numismatic items.

'(6) ISSUANCE-

'(A) QUALITY OF COINS- The Secretary may mint and issue such number of quarter dollars of each design selected under paragraph (3) in uncirculated and proof qualities as the Secretary determines to be appropriate.

'(B) SILVER COINS- Notwithstanding subsection (b), the Secretary may mint and issue such number of quarter dollars of each design selected under paragraph (3) as the Secretary determines to be appropriate, with a content of 90 percent silver and 10 percent copper.

'(7) PERIOD OF ISSUANCE-

'(A) IN GENERAL- Subject to paragraph (2), the program established under this subsection shall continue in effect until a national site in each State has been honored.

'(B) SECOND ROUND AT DISCRETION OF SECRETARY-

'(i) DETERMINATION- The Secretary may make a determination before the end of the 9-year period beginning when the first quarter dollar is issued under this subsection to continue the period of issuance until a second national site in each State, the District of Columbia, and each territory referred to in this subsection has been honored with a design on a quarter dollar.

'(ii) NOTICE AND REPORT- Within 30 days after making a determination under clause (i), the Secretary shall submit a written report on such determination to the Committee on Financial Services of the House of Representatives and the Committee on Banking, Housing, and Urban Affairs of the Senate.

'(iii) APPLICABILITY OF PROVISIONS- If the Secretary makes a determination under clause (i), the provisions of this subsection applicable to site and design selection and approval, the order, timing, and conditions of issuance shall apply in like manner as the initial issuance of quarter dollars under this subsection, except that the issuance of quarter dollars pursuant to such determination bearing the first design shall commence in order immediately following the last issuance of quarter dollars under the first round.

'(iv) CONTINUATION UNTIL ALL STATES ARE HONORED- If the Secretary makes a determination under clause (i), the program under this subsection shall continue until a second site in each State has been so honored.

'(8) DESIGNS AFTER END OF PROGRAM- Upon the completion of the coin program under this subsection, the design on--

'(A) the obverse of the quarter dollar shall revert to the same design containing an image of President Washington in effect for the quarter dollar before the institution of the 50-State quarter dollar program; and

'(B) notwithstanding the fourth sentence of subsection (d) (1), the reverse of the quarter dollar shall contain an image of General Washington crossing the Delaware River prior to the Battle of Trenton.

'(9) NATIONAL SITE- For purposes of this subsection, the term 'national site' means any site under the supervision, management, or conservancy of the National Park Service, the United States Forest Service, the United States Fish and Wildlife Service, or any similar department or agency of the Federal Government, including any national park, national monument, national battlefield, national military park, national historical park, national historic site, national lakeshore, seashore, recreation area, parkway, scenic river, or trail and any site in the National Wildlife Refuge System.

'(10) APPLICATION IN EVENT OF INDEPENDENCE- If any territory becomes independent or otherwise ceases to be a territory or possession of the United States before quarter dollars bearing designs which are emblematic of such territory are minted pursuant to this subsection, this subsection shall cease to apply with respect to such territory.'

TITLE II--BULLION INVESTMENT PRODUCTS

SEC. 201. SILVER BULLION COIN.

Section 5112 of title 31, United States Code, is amended by inserting after subsection (t) (as added by title I of this Act) the following new subsection:

'(u) Silver Bullion Investment Product-

'(1) IN GENERAL- The Secretary shall strike and make available for sale such number of bullion coins as the Secretary determines to be appropriate that are exact duplicates of the quarter dollars issued under subsection (t), each of which shall--

'(A) have a diameter of 3.0 inches and weigh 5.0 ounces;

'(B) contain .999 fine silver;

'(C) have incused into the edge the fineness and weight of the bullion coin;

'(D) bear an inscription of the denomination of such coin, which shall be 'quarter dollar'; and

'(E) not be minted or issued by the United States Mint as so-called 'fractional' bullion coins or in any size other than the size described in paragraph (A).

'(2) AVAILABILITY FOR SALE- Bullion coins minted under paragraph (1)--

'(A) shall become available for sale no sooner than the first day of the calendar year in which the circulating quarter dollar of which such bullion coin is a duplicate is issued; and

'(B) may only be available for sale during the year in which such circulating quarter dollar is issued.

'(3) DISTRIBUTION-

'(A) IN GENERAL- In addition to the authorized dealers utilized by the Secretary in distributing bullion coins and solely for purposes of distributing bullion coins issued under this subsection, the Director of the National Park Service, or the designee of the Director, may purchase numismatic items issued under this subsection, but only in units of no fewer than 1,000 at a time, and the Director, or the Director's designee, may resell or repackage such numismatic items as the Director determines to be appropriate.

'(B) RESALE- The Director of the National Park Service, or the designee of the Director, may resell, at cost and without repackaging, numismatic items acquired by the Director or such designee under subparagraph (A) to any party affiliated with any national site honored by a quarter dollar under subsection (t) for repackaging and resale by such party in the same manner and to the same extent as such party would be authorized to engage in such activities under subparagraph (A) if the party were acting as the designee of the Director under such subparagraph.'

Speaker of the House of Representatives.

Vice President of the United States and

President of the Senate.

Hot Springs

Date: 2010
State: Arkansas
Issue: 1 of 56
Mintmarks: P, D & S

Mintage and Pricing

YEAR	MM	MINTAGE	AUCTION	GRADE	PRICE ($)
2010	P	35,600,000	8 May, 2011	NGC 67	85
2010	D	34,000,000	4 Oct, 2011	PCGS 66	8
2010	Collector	27,000			
2010	Unc. Bullion	33,000	3 Apr, 2011	PCGS 68	500
2010	S (proof)	1,222,966	13 Mar, 2011	PCGS 70	42
2010	S (silver)	693,403	2 Jan, 2011	PCGS 70	110

Obverse

Bust of George Washington by John Flanagan in 1932 (based on Jean-Antoine Houdon's statue circa 1790). Above Washington's bust reads UNITED STATES OF AMERICA. Beneath his chin reads LIBERTY. Beside his hair braid is the national motto IN GOD WE TRUST. Below his neckline reads QUARTER DOLLAR. On the side of his neckline are John Flanagan's initials JF.

Reverse

Edge: Unmilled; incused with .999 FINE SILVER 5 OUNCE. Reverse at top (L to R) reads NATIONAL HOT SPRINGS; bottom (L to R) reads ARKANSAS, 2010, and the motto E PLURIBUS UNUM.

Designed by Don Everhart (U.S. Mint) and engraved by Joseph Menna, the reverse features the façade of the Hot Springs National Park headquarters building with a thermal fountain in the background. The headquarters was built in a Spanish colonial style and completed in 1936.

About the Featured National Park

The eight-square miles that comprise Hot Springs National Park were established as a national site in 1832 to conserve the 47 springs from Hot Springs Mountain.

Located in an urban area, early residents worried the push of progress would destroy the beauty of the natural hot springs. President Andrew Jackson agreed, designating Hot Springs National Park as the first federally protected park in the country.

Magnificent bath houses were built to offer visitors the opportunity to enjoy the springs' therapeutic benefits. Eight bath houses remain today, though only two are currently in operation.

Grading Hints

The high points of the coin's obverse are prone to contact marks. The field off Washington's nose and behind head curls and behind head curls are also prone to contact marks. Reverse: the imaginary centerline from "p" in springs to "20" is the high point that takes contact marks and wear.

Design finalists for the Hot Springs National
Park quarter.

Notes from the Citizens Coinage Advisory Committee

The Advisory Committee met 9/22/09 with the following findings: "For the coin representing Hot Springs National Park in Arkansas, members appreciated the sense of perspective on Arkansas design one, though the design was overall considered to be too intricate for the small palette of a coin, as was design three. Design four was appreciated for its inclusion of natural landscape, and for its clear focus on the fountain as the site's primary attraction.

For Arkansas the committee recommended design four, which received 24 points. Design three received 11 points." On 9/29/09 the CCAC wrote to Treasury Secretary Tim Geithner: "For the coin portraying Hot Springs National Park in Arkansas, the Committee strongly recommends design four, which shows a focused view of the public fountain in front of the site's headquarters building. Members appreciated the design's clear imagery, emphasis on water, and incorporation of natural landscape."

Notes from the Commission of Fine Arts

The CFA met on 9/17/09 in Washington D.C.

Ms. Budow: *We worked very closely with the superintendents of the particular sites, Hot Springs and Grand Canyon, et cetera, and they informed us as to which designs they thought would be most emblematic and appropriate to be on the coin and then photographs to support those designs. So, yes; they were primarily based on photographs. And we took a lot of, like I said, guidance from the superintendents' offices as to what they thought was most important in honoring that site on the quarter.*

It is a little bit different from the process in the 50 State Quarters Program.

So, starting with No. 01, it shows an angled view of a Stevens balustrade with a fountain in the central bay and a Fordyce bath house to the right. The entrance to the balustrade situated between Fordyce and Maurice bath houses has eagle-top columns, which are designed to be the formal entrance to Hot Springs Reservation and is located in the middle of the bath-house row.

The balustrade is named for Lieutenant Robert Stevens, the Army engineer, who designed the entrances to the reservation and conceived of the magnolia-line promenade along the front of the row. Fordyce bath house currently operates as a visitor center and museum. So that is No. 01.

No. 02 depicts a close-up view of the entrance to Hot Springs National Park Headquarters Building with the fountain in the foreground. The headquarters building is a Spanish Colonial Revival, two-story, rectangular block building with simplified Baroque Revival treatment to the door and facade with a tower roof and decorative brackets, brick wall, iron grills and symmetrical casement windows and French doors. It was built in 1935 and completed in 1936. It actually has the National Park's symbol there and that front one.

Ms. Nelson: *That would be as big as the head of a pin, the park symbol? Actually, what we got on the printout, this looks elongated. I don't know. Maybe it is a screen. It looks a little different proportion.*

Ms. Budow: *Maybe it seems a bit stretched on the screen. It is definitely going to be the regular quarter size.*

No. 03 is sort of a variation featuring an angle view of the entrance, again to the Hot Springs National Park Headquarters Building with the fountain in the foreground showing some more details of the Headquarters Building. The park did feel it is important to show a water feature. That is something they did mention to us. No. 04, sort of zoomed in view of the fountain in front of the Headquarters Building.

Ms. Balmori: *Would it not be better if we saw all of these in the sense that are talking about the issue of creating a template in how they are done rather than going about choosing one? I think that somehow the choices that have been made about this are not the right choices.*

Ms Nelson: *This is the template, the inscriptions on the outside; right?*

Ms Budow: *So that circle you saw that is inside of the "Hot Springs, Arkansas," "E Pluribus Unum," that whole center area will be recessed and the design inside of it, then, will be raised above that level. So it will be very different for us and we think it will be sculpturally more interesting.*

Ms. Plater-Zyberk: *What Diana is bringing up I think might be worth just a quick look-through the—*

Ms Nelson: *The other parks.*

Ms. Plater-Zyberk: *Because one of the questions I think that comes up, and this one is whether you want that template to exist, the ring, especially because it becomes a straight line across the bottom and that sets up some problems with the images.*

Ms. Balmori: *It does set up a problem.*

Ms. Budow: *All the designs we have are in the same template.*

Ms. Plater-Zyberk: *Is this a template that is already being used so we shouldn't even be discussing it?*

Ms. Budow: *No; it is what we are proposing to use for the program.*

Ms. Balmori: *Then I would certainly suggest that you get a complete circle and don't do the flat line at the bottom. It is just very awkward.*

Ms. Plater-Zyberk: *I agree. And, if we are staying on this one, then I would—the second one seems to be the simplest one.*

Ms. Nelson: *That's what I like.*

Mr. Powell: *Yes; I like that, too.*

Ms. Plater-Zyberk: *Although one of the things, like you said, that the wall signage might be—*

Ms. Nelson: *Be lost.*

Ms. Plater-Zyberk: *—superfluous because you really won't see it. It will just look like a smudge. If the circle is completed, then kind of that bad intersection of the base of the fountain and the flat line of the circle will go away.*

Ms. Balmori: *But, apart from that, in this particular case, all four are really quite awkward drawings, awkward presentations. I also go for 02 because it is the simplest, but—*

Mr. Powell: *I think we have got a motion for 02.*

Ms. Balmori: *—it doesn't do any honor to Hot Springs. It needs another sort of drawing. I am just wondering if there is a good photograph that can be interpreted better than this.*

Mr. Powell: *I like No. 02 also if it can be made—so the perspective doesn't flatten it all out.*

Ms. Nelson: *Right.*

Mr. Powell: *But, yes; I would go for 02.*

Yellowstone

Date: 2010
State: Wyoming
Issue: 2 of 56
Mintmarks: P, D & S

Mintage and Pricing

YEAR	MM	MINTAGE	AUCTION	GRADE	PRICE ($)
2010	P	33,600,000		NGC 69	130
2010	D	34,800,000		PCGS 67	24
2010	Unc. Bullion	33,000		NGC 69	2,530
2010	S (proof)	1,222,966	16 Jan 2011	PCGS 70	120
2010	S (silver)	693,000		PCGS 70	120

Obverse

Bust of George Washington by John Flanagan in 1932 (based on Jean-Antoine Houdon's statue circa 1790). Above Washington's bust reads UNITED STATES OF AMERICA. Beneath his chin reads LIBERTY. Beside his hair braid is the national motto IN GOD WE TRUST. Below his neckline reads QUARTER DOLLAR. On the side of his neckline are John Flanagan's initials JF.

Reverse

Edge: Unmilled; incused with .999 FINE SILVER 5 OUNCE. Reverse at top (L to R) reads YELLOWSTONE; bottom (L to R) reads WYOMING, 2010, and the motto E PLURIBUS UNUM.

Designed and engraved by Don Everhart II, the reverse features Old Faithful Geyser with a mature bull bison in the foreground.

About the Featured National Park

At 2.2 million acres of land, mostly in Wyoming but covering parts of Montana and Idaho, Yellowstone is comprised of magnificent lakes, rivers, waterfalls, canyons and mountain ranges. Yellowstone Caldera, the largest supervolcano on the continent, fuels the park's geothermal activity, which includes Old Faithful, one of the world's most extraordinary geysers. Grizzly bears, bison and elk are but a few of the hundreds of species of wildlife found here.

Yellowstone, the first national park in the U.S., is widely considered to be the first one in the world. Visitors enjoy hiking, sightseeing, camping, boating and fishing.

Grading Hints

The high points of the coin's obverse are prone to contact marks. The field off Washington's nose and behind head curls are prone to contact marks. Reverse: Most of these coins are in higher grades. From circulation, the high points—bison's nose and upper portions of rippling geyser—are most likely to show wear.

WY-01

WY-02

WY-03

Design finalists for the Yellowstone National
Park quarter.

Notes from the Citizens Coinage Advisory Committee

On 9/22/09, the CCAC met and discussed the proposed designs. "For the coin representing Yellowstone National Park in Wyoming, members criticized the representation of Old Faithful on design three as unrealistic, and felt that the lodge in design two distracted from the geyser. Members generally spoke highly of design one, for its inclusion of the parks' wildlife as a complement to the iconic geyser image."

Mitch Sanders, chair, wrote to Secretary Geithner with the Committee's recommendations on 9/30/09: "For the coin portraying Yellowstone National Park in Wyoming, the Committee strongly prefers design one, showing Old Faithful geyser with bison in the foreground and background. Members felt that design one would work well on a small coin, and that the depiction of animal life enhanced the design."

Notes from the Commission of Fine Arts

On 9/17/09, the CFA met and discussed the Yellowstone coin. The discussion was lively, and, in a word, the committee members were not happy with the designs or the process.

Ms. Budow: *Moving on to Yellowstone, established in 1872, Yellowstone National Park is home to a large variety of wildlife including grizzly bears, wolves, bison and elk. Preserved within the park are Old Faithful and a collection of the world's most extraordinary geysers and the Grand Canyon of the Yellowstone.*

Starting with No. 01, we have the Old Faithful Geyser in the background with a mature bull bison in the foreground. There is another bison, of course, to the right in the background.

No. 02 features the geyser with the Old Faithful Inn. Old Faithful Inn is a masterpiece of rustic architecture in its stylized design and fine craftsmanship. Its influence on American architecture, particularly park architecture, was immeasurable. The building is a rustic log and wood-frame structure with gigantic proportions nearly 700-feet in length and seven-stories high.

No. 03 depicts a large gathering of visitors to Yellowstone admiring Old Faithful with the lodgepole pine forest in the background. I know the geysers kind of look like clouds, but, again, that is for sculptural reasons.

And later:

Ms. Nelson: *My feeling is keep trying on this one. I don't think there is anything that has Yellowstone—I just don't think we have any—*
Ms. Balmori: *I don't either. There is an extraordinary photo of Weston of precisely the springs coming up and Old Faithful. It is an extraordinarily poetic image. Why can't they use a good photograph.*
Ms. Budow: *Well, we worked with Yellowstone. We worked with the park and these are the images that they preferred and they thought were the best.*
Ms. Balmori: *They have done badly. They have done very badly by themselves.*
Mr. Rybczynski: *I think this is going to come up all the time. I think commemorating national parks on quarters is really a bad idea. I just want*

to get that on the record. It is a daunting task for a designer to take a vastness of something like this and put it on this. It probably sounded good when some politician thought of it but, in practice, it is going to be a real struggle and we are going to have 50 of these conversations because it is going to be impossible to show the vastness, which is what we all remember about national parks, on a quarter.

Ms. Plater-Zyberk: *But we are not going to roll back the legislation and make—*

Mr. Rybczynski: *No; I just want to get it on the record because I am just really unhappy with all of these. It is not because they are bad coin designers; I think they have been given an impossible job.*

Ms. Balmori: *I disagree with that statement. I just think there is a way of getting vastness on a small thing if—and there are examples of incredible good photographs of the west that I have seen just printed very small and I have been astounded at how they could capture the vastness.*

The national parks are incredibly emblematic of our country so I just think that being put on a coin is a good idea. But I really do think that we have to choose incredibly good artists, and I don't think that each one of the parks selecting its own image is a very good idea.

Yosemite

Date: 2010
State: California
Issue: 3 of 56
Mintmarks: P, D & S

Mintage and Pricing

YEAR	MM	MINTAGE	AUCTION	GRADE	PRICE ($)
2010	P	24,800,000	22 Mar 2011	ANACS 67	10
2010	D	35,200,000	20 Feb 2011	ANACS 67	6
2010	Unc. Bullion	33,000	1 May 2011	NGC 69	719
2010	S (proof)	1,222,966	13 Mar 2011	PCGS 70	25
2010	S (silver)	693,403	2 Dec 2011	PCGS 60	65

Obverse

Bust of George Washington by John Flanagan in 1932 (based on Jean-Antoine Houdon's statue circa 1790). Above Washington's bust reads UNITED STATES OF AMERICA. Beneath his chin reads LIBERTY. Beside his hair braid is the national motto IN GOD WE TRUST. Below his neckline reads QUARTER DOLLAR. On the side of his neckline are John Flanagan's initials JF.

Reverse

Edge: Unmilled; incused with .999 FINE SILVER 5 OUNCE. Reverse at top (L to R) reads YOSEMITE; bottom (L to R) reads CALIFORNIA, 2010, and the motto E PLURIBUS UNUM.

Designed by Joseph Menna (U.S. Mint) and engraved by Phebe Hemphill (U.S. Mint), the reverse features the iconic El Capitan, which rises more than 3,000 feet above the valley floor and is the largest monolith of granite in the world.

About the Featured National Park

Yosemite National Park's nearly 1,200 square miles offer lush, narrow valleys densely packed with pine trees and surrounded by spectacular granite cliffs in the western Sierra Nevadas. Its giant sequoias are the world's largest trees in terms of volume, growing upwards of 280 feet and 25 feet in diameter.

Established as a national site in 1890, 3.7 million visitors annually spend their time primarily in Yosemite Valley. In addition to the famous El Capitan and Half Dome summits, Yosemite Falls is North America's tallest waterfall.

Grading Hints

The high points of the coin's obverse are prone to contact marks. The field off Washington's nose and behind head curls are prone to contact marks. Reverse: log in the foreground and tree, atop of El Capitan, treeline at left (lower) is likely to show wear. On circulated coins, incused mottos.

CA-01

CA-02

CA-03

CA-04

Design finalists for the Yosemite National Park
quarter.

Notes from the Citizens Coinage Advisory Committee

From the minutes of the 9/22/09 meeting: "For California the committee recommended design three, which received 18 points. Design two received 11 points."

Participating: John Alexander, Doreen Bolger, Michael Brown, Arthur Houghton, Gary Marks, Rick Meier, Mitch Sanders (Chairperson), Donald Scarinci, Joe Winter (via telephone). Sept. 30 letter to Secretary of the Treasury Geithner: "For the coin portraying Yosemite National Park in California, the Committee prefers design three, featuring a view of El Capitan. Members praised the simplicity and ruggedness of the design, and its effective composition."

Notes from the Commission of Fine Arts

This design depicts Yosemite Falls, the upper falls, the central cascade and the lower falls with the black bear in the foreground. I want to make sure that the Lost Arrow Spire is depicted up at the top adjacent to the falls.

No. 02 features Yosemite Falls again with a Stellar's jaybird perched on a branch in the foreground.

No. 03 shows the distinctive El Capitan rising more than 3,000 feet above the valley floor, the largest monolith of granite in the world. It is a favorite among experienced rock climbers.

And No. 04 shows Half Dome with the forest in the foreground. Half Dome is, perhaps, the most recognized symbol of Yosemite rising nearly 5,000 feet above the valley floor, one of the most sought-after landmarks in Yosemite.

Ms. Balmori: *Could I ask you a question? With Yosemite I am particularly familiar and I also know all of the great photographs of Yosemite. Is there an issue of copyright if you were to use some of the great photographs of Yosemite?*

Ms. Budow: *Yes; that can be an issue for us. We have to make sure the images are in the public domain, that we have the rights to the photographs. Yes; so these images were provided by the park and they are owned by the park so they don't have any constraints. It is an issue for us with all our designs, actually.*

Mr. Powell: *I think 04 is a good design, but it looks like it is—*

Ms. Balmori: *Badly drawn.*

Mr. Powell: *—an unfinished drawing almost.*

Ms. Plater-Zyberk: *Is your memory of El Capitan from that angle?*

Ms. Balmori: *A very different El Capitan.*

Ms. Plater-Zyberk: *A different angle.*

Mr. Powell: *Ansel Adams' image of Yosemite is the iconic—*

Ms. Balmori: *It is iconic. It is totally iconic.*

Ms. Plater-Zyberk: *It just feels as if all of—even the next one we are going to see is that they are trying to give you a new image of it rather than the classic.*

Ms. Balmori: *This isn't the way.*

Ms. Nelson: *Again, you have trouble with the flatness.*

Ms. Plater-Zyberk: *Yes.*

Ms. Nelson: *You need to make it a complete circle rather than that--*

Mr. Powell: *No. 01 is also a very recognizable—for Yosemite. I never much associated black bears with Yosemite the way you do grizzlies with Yellowstone.*

Ms. Budow: *There are only black bears. The grizzlies are, I think, extinct in that area.*

Mr. Powell: *I think if you can get El Capitan right, El Capitan is the right subject.*

Ms. Balmori: *Yes.*

Ms. Plater-Zyberk: *Yes.*

Ms. Nelson: *That would be the simplest.*

Ms. Balmori: *You might investigate if Ansel Adams' image is available because he has done the definitive image of it.*

Mr. Powell: *So I would move 04.*

Ms. Nelson: *04 with refinements.*

Mr. Luebke: *I'm sorry; 04 is the—*

Ms. Budow: *04 is the Half Dome. 03 is El Capitan.*

Mr. Powell: *Yes. Half Dome with refinement.*

Ms. Budow: *Okay.*

Mr. Powell: *04.*

Ms. Plater-Zyberk: *I'm sorry; I think I renamed it. I'm sorry.*

Mr. Powell: *With the correct name.*

Ms. Nelson: *Half Dome. Okay.*

Grand Canyon

Date: 2010
State: Arizona
Issue: 4 of 56
Mintmarks: P, D & S

Mintage and Pricing

YEAR	MM	MINTAGE	AUCTION	GRADE	PRICE ($)
2010	P	35,400,000	1 Dec 2011	PCGS 67	39
2010	D	35,600,000	31 Oct 2011	PCGS 67	55
2010	Unc. Bullion	33,000	20 Mar 2011	PCGS 69	625
2010	S (proof)	1,222,966	13 Mar 2011	PCGS 70	70
2010	S (silver)	693,403	7 Feb 2011	PCGS 70	120

Obverse

Bust of George Washington by John Flanagan in 1932 (based on Jean-Antoine Houdon's statue circa 1790). Above Washington's bust reads UNITED STATES OF AMERICA. Beneath his chin reads LIBERTY. Beside his hair braid is the national motto IN GOD WE TRUST. Below his neckline reads QUARTER DOLLAR. On the side of his neckline are John Flanagan's initials JF.

Reverse

Edge: Unmilled; incused with .999 FINE SILVER 5 OUNCE. Reverse at top (L to R) reads GRAND CANYON; bottom (L to R) reads ARIZONA, 2010, and the motto E PLURIBUS UNUM.

Designed and engraved by Phebe Hemphill (U.S. Mint), the reverse features a view of the granaries above the Nankoweap Delta in Marble Canyon near the Colorado River. Marble Canyon is the northernmost section of the Grand Canyon. Granaries were used for storing food and seeds (A.D. 500).

About the Featured National Park

President Theodore Roosevelt used his power under the Antiquities Act of 1906 to set aside more than 800,000 acres at Grand Canyon, which became a national park in 1919, three years after the National Park Service was formed.

The sheer enormity of Grand Canyon, 277-river-miles long, up to 18 miles wide and a mile deep, is awe-inspiring. Some visitors attempt to capture its breadth by taking helicopter tours, but it is perhaps more fun to explore the old-fashioned way, hiking on one of the canyon's many trails. Even if you never make it all the way to the bottom, it's an experience you'll never forget.

Grading Hints

The high points of the coin's obverse are prone to contact marks. The field off Washington's nose and behind head curls are prone to contact marks. Reverse: axis of Grand Canyon's east wall granaries above the Nankoweap Delta in Marble Canyon near the Colorado River.

AZ-01

AZ-02

AZ-03

AZ-04

Design finalists for the Grand Canyon
National Park quarter.

Notes from the Citizens Coinage Advisory Committee

Letter to Treasury Secy. Tim Geithner 9/30/09: 'For the coin portraying Grand Canyon National Park in Arizona, the Committee narrowly prefers design one, featuring a canyon-level view of the granaries above the Nankoweap Delta, over design four, which features an aerial view of the canyon. Both were considered to be powerful images, with design one preferred for its more immediate, human-scaled view of the canyon."

Meeting 9/22/09 minutes: "For the coin representing Grand Canyon National Park in Arizona, discussion centered around designs one and four, which offered the clearest depictions of the majesty of the canyon. Although there was some concern that the person walking along the trail would be so small as to be indistinct, design one appealed to many committee members for its up-close, human-scaled depiction of the canyon."

Notes from the Commission of Fine Arts

The CFA met 9/17/09 where the Mint began to go through the designs one by one.

"This features a view of the granaries above the Nankoweap Delta in Marble Canyon near the Colorado River. Granaries were used for storing food and seeds by ancient people. They are also looking for a distinctive design from the Grand Canyon image we had on the 50 State Quarters design.

No. 02 features a view of the Grand Canyon with a bighorn sheep in the foreground.

No. 03 shows a view with the Grand Canyon cedar tree in the foreground.

And No. 04 is just more of an aerial view."

Then came questions from the Commissioners.

Ms. Nelson: *Do you have a reminder of what the Grand Canyon quarter was for Arizona?*
Ms. Budow: *It had sort of a banner in it that said Grand Canyon State and it had a—I am trying to think of the name now. It had a certain tree that didn't grow in the Grand Canyon. That is why it was separated by the actual—*
Mr. Luebke: *We could pull it out of the display.*
Ms. Nelson: *I was just wondering.*
Ms. Budow: *It is more of a classic image.*
Ms. Balmori: *Wouldn't it have to be a sort of modern coin with a modern rendering of the Grand Canyon? I was thinking of the photographs of David Hockney of the Grand Canyon which are so extraordinary. I was thinking you could jump a generation of forms of representation of the Grand Canyon. But—*
Ms. Nelson: *I think it is too tiny to do that.*
Ms. Budow: *No. 01, I think there is actually a little hiker up there on the right side. It is hard to make out.*

Ms. Balmori: *No; I think it could be done.*

Mr. Powell: *I prefer 01.*

Ms. Nelson: *I think 01, if you have a different template, it is not going to be so awkward. That would work. That would give you the feeling.*

Ms. Plater-Zyberk: *And the foregrounds, I think, are always difficult and that slag heap.*

Ms. Balmori: *Yes; it is a horrible slag heap.*

Ms. Plater-Zyberk: *It is not clear what that is. Is it rocks or a pile of dirt.*

Mr. Powell: *Do you like the bighorns?*

Ms. Plater-Zyberk: *And I think the animals in the foreground set up a kind of theme. Do you do that in each park?*

Ms. Balmori: *They are horrible.*

Ms. Budow: *We try to include animals sometimes if they were very distinct to that park, again to differentiate it from another park. So, the foreground will have much higher relief and the background a lower relief to give it that perception of depth.*

Mr. Powell: *I could go with 04.*

Ms. Plater-Zyberk: *But if 01, just some attention is paid to that foreground which takes up a quarter almost of the image—*

Ms. Balmori: *Yes.*

Ms. Plater-Zyberk: *I think that what is interesting about it is the depth.*

Mr. Powell: *I like that, too.*

Ms. Plater-Zyberk: *So maybe just saying watch out for the—*

Ms. Balmori: *But something would have to be done with the foreground. I agree with you.*

Mr. Powell: *Then No. 01 with some refinement if that can, in fact, happen.*

Ms. Plater-Zyberk: *It actually might be moving the view slightly so that the foreground isn't at the halfway point. The vertical line is right in the middle of the coin and maybe it should be more to the right so that view of the depth is larger and then that foreground will also shrink.*

Ms. Balmori: *Agreed.*

Mr. Powell: *And the idea of No. 01 with some—*

Ms. Budow: *Sort of shifting it.*

Mr. Powell: *—perspective adjustments.*

Ms. Balmori: *It needs work on that foreground.*

Mr. Powell: *Or words to that effect.*

Ms. Budow: *Okay.*

Ms. Balmori: *And it needs the circle at the bottom instead of a straight line.*

Mr. Powell: *Motion?*

Ms. Plater-Zyberk: *So moved.*

Mr. Powell: *Second.*

Ms. Balmori: *Second.*

Mr. Powell: *All in favor of the Grand Canyon?*

[Chorus of ayes.]

Ms. Nelson: *No. 01 with adjustments.*

Mr. Luebke: *We will include general language regarding the template to recommend strongly about the continuing circle.*

Ms. Balmori: *Yes.*

Ms. Nelson: *Each design would benefit.*

Mr. Powell: *The more you look at it, the more obvious it should be that the template should be a circular one, I think.*

Mount Hood

Date: 2010
State: Oregon
Issue: 5 of 56
Mintmarks: P, D & S

Mintage and Pricing

YEAR	MM	MINTAGE	AUCTION	GRADE	PRICE ($)
2010	P	34,400,000	8 May 2011	NGC 69	160
2010	D	34,400,000	8 May 2011	NGC 67	190
2010	Collector	25,592			
2010	Unc. Bullion	33,000	13 Sep 2011	PCGS 68	310
2010	S (proof)	1,222,966	1 Aug 2010	PCGS 70	75
2010	S (silver)	693,403	13 Sep 2010	PCGS 70	140

Obverse

Bust of George Washington by John Flanagan in 1932 (based on Jean-Antoine Houdon's statue circa 1790). Above Washington's bust reads UNITED STATES OF AMERICA. Beneath his chin reads LIBERTY. Beside his hair braid is the national motto IN GOD WE TRUST. Below his neckline reads QUARTER DOLLAR. On the side of his neckline are John Flanagan's initials JF.

Reverse

Edge: Unmilled; incused with .999 FINE SILVER 5 OUNCE. Reverse at top (L to R) reads MOUNT HOOD; bottom (L to R) reads OREGON, 2010, and the motto E PLURIBUS UNUM.

Designed and engraved by Phebe Hemphill (U.S. Mint), the reverse features a view of Mount Hood with Lost Lake in the foreground.

About the Featured National Park

Mount Hood National Forest encompasses more than 60 miles of gorgeous mountains, lakes and streams in the Northern Willamette Valley, just 20 miles east of Portland. The rugged landscape around the Klakamath Wild and Scenic River gives visitors the sensation of being in the Old West.

The Timberland Lodge is a national historic site that is open year round. The resort offers alpine skiing, snowboarding, cross country skiing, hiking, music festivals and fine dining.

Grading Hints

The high points of the coin's obverse are prone to contact marks. The field off Washington's nose and behind head curls are prone to contact marks. Reverse: The peak of Mount Hood will show wear along with the south east ridge.

OR-01

OR-02

OR-03

OR-04

Design finalists for the Mount Hood National
Park quarter.

Notes from the Citizens Coinage Advisory Committee

Minutes of 9/22/09: "For the coin representing Mount Hood National Forest in Oregon, several members were adamantly opposed to the inclusion of the Portland skyline, which was considered to detract from the image of Mount Hood. The view of the mountain on designs three and four was preferred to that on designs one and two, though the rhododendron on design four was considered to be extraneous. For Oregon the committee recommended design three, which received 27 points. Designs one and four each received three points."

9/30/2009 (Mitch Saunders, chairman to Geithner, Treasury Secretary: "For the coin portraying Mount Hood National Forest in

Oregon, the Committee overwhelmingly prefers design three, featuring a view of Mount Hood with Lost Lake in the foreground. Design three was lauded for the artistry of its imagery, and for the absence of design elements that would detract from the view of the mountain."

Notes from the Commission of Fine Arts

Design No. 01 features the east side of Mount Hood with an orchard in the foreground, specifically the Hood River Valley Orchard country east of Mount Hood. The area above the orchard is meant to represent the foothills of the forest area.

No. 02 features the west side of Mount Hood with the Portland skyline in the foreground. Again, the foothills are depicted. The mountain comes out of the foothills of the forest.

Ms. Nelson: *Powell's Bookstore is right down there.*

Ms. Budow: *No. 03 shows a view of Mount Hood and Lost Lake in the foreground.*

Actually, No. 04 is very similar. It just has the addition of the local rhododendron along the inner rim which is a local flower.

Those are the four designs for Mount Hood.

Ms. Plater-Zyberk: *I think the one that probably would come across in the most simple way is 03. But No. 02 is appealing to me just because it is, among the parks, the one that is very closely related to a city.*

Ms. Balmori: *But it is so badly rendered. It is so badly done.*

Mr. Powell: *I like 03.*

Ms. Plater-Zyberk: *No. 03?*

Mr. Powell: *Well, just as a design. I think that is the cleanest of the three, of the four.*

Ms. Nelson: *When I did this at home, I picked 03.*

Ms. Plater-Zyberk: *May I make a motion for 03?*

Mr. Powell: *Certainly.*

Ms. Balmori: *I will have to abstain. This is not satisfying at all.*

Mr. Powell: *Is there a second? I will second 03. We have an abstention.*

Ms. Nelson: *A lukewarm.*

Mr. Powell: *A lukewarm enthusiasm for 03. But I need, if you please, at least up or down on it. One abstention. I will vote for it.*

Ms. Plater-Zyberk: *I vote for it.*

Ms. Nelson: *I vote for 03.*

Mr. Belle: *I can vote for it.*

Mr. Powell: *Is that a "can" for it? You can? Yes; that was a "can."*

Mr. Powell: *Then No. 03 with my colleague's abstention.*

Ms. Budow: *That concludes our presentation. Thank you so much for your time.*

Ms. Nelson: *I would like to ask one question.*

Mr. Belle: *May I ask the Mint's representative—I am curious to know, you have appeared before us now for a number of times over the last years. I am curious to know how many of the recommendations that we have made to you actually changed the design of any of the coins that you have submitted to us.*

Ms. Budow: *We would have to go back and take a look but your comments are always seriously considered.*

Mr. Belle: *Yes. That is not what I said. I said, "actually changed" the coinage.*

Mr. Powell: *Well, they are still round.*

Ms. Nelson: *They are still round.*

Ms. Budow: *I am think offhand of some designs that CFA recommended versus the other committee and we went with the CFA's recommendation. I can't think right off the top of the my head of an alteration or a rendition, but I am sure I could provide that information for you.*

Mr. Powell: *There are some I recognize in your catalogue that we approved. But, numerically, I don't—*

Ms. Nelson: *One thing I was going to—we have looked at Mr. Moy's medal twice and he had the Renaissance Man, the Michelangelo. It is still going with that even though we recommended not to.*

Ms. Budow: *That is currently on hold, that project.*

Ms. Nelson: *It is on hold? Okay. I was just curious.*

Mr. Powell: *And Mr. Borlaug, Byron Nelson.*

Ms. Budow: *He just passed away and luckily he got his Congressional Gold Medal in I think 2007.*

Mr. Powell: *Is this double eagle the subject of the controversy over those ones that were just discovered in a safe-deposit box?*

Ms. Budow: *I am not familiar with that story, so I would have to go back.*

Mr. Powell: *It was in the paper yesterday.*

Ms. Plater-Zyberk: *That is a question of curiosity, but it also might be a great usefulness to, at some point, have a report back and perhaps a few examples of where our comments were useful and a change was made and* then a few examples of where they couldn't be followed and, in reality, for what reasons because I think—

Ms. Balmori: *We need some feedback.*

Ms. Plater-Zyberk: *I think none of us are—we are designers of many things but not coins. We don't necessarily understand the method. You tried to educate us with a white paper a while ago, but I think, knowing how these things land, we see it in the other project because we see them being done around the city.*

Ms. Budow: *I think it was about a year ago—I can also check with the Secretary and the Assistant Secretary—but we had a meeting, an admin meeting, and we went over some of the designs. That may be something we could look to introduce again.*

Mr. Powell: *I think it would be very helpful.*

Ms. Budow: *We showed some of the designs then that the CFA had recommended, what the finals were, which ones were in consideration, and kind of walk you through the process of, again, the line art instructions we give to the artist and—*

Mr. Luebke: *This is a recurring issue, obviously, for several years. And we have gone through a number of consultations. In fact, we went through a fairly exhaustive look just recently in January when actually you evaluated what the last—some series—*

Ms. Budow: *Earlier this year; correct.*

Mr. Luebke: *In any case, we haven't had anything where they actually had a specific tallying of how these were issued consistently with the Commission's recommendations, or these were changed and this was somewhere in between.*

We can request that. I don't know if they will be able to provide that, but we can certainly request it.

Ms. Plater-Zyberk: *I am not sure the tally is important as much as some examples.*

Mr. Powell: *Just maybe some examples.*

Ms. Budow: *We can pull it together.*

Mr. Powell: *Just some jpgs would be—*

Ms. Budow: *The recommendations go to the Secretary of the Treasury for his final decision, comments of the CFA and the CCC, all their comments are included in that memorandum as well as your letter.*

Mr. Belle: *I think, the general question, given the amount of time we spend reviewing your designs is a considerable amount of time. I think we* *can't be faulted for sometimes believing that those recommendations just fall off into the.... They just disappear. We certainly don't see any results.*

Ms. Budow: *We can get back to you with some examples. But I can think of changes we have made. I just can't think of them right off-hand. And, definitely, your recommendations were—*

Mr. Powell: *It would help if we were all given complementary copies of the—*

Ms. Nelson: *I think the trouble with the quarter design was the governors had the final say and a lot of them didn't have aesthetic—they just had to satisfy every county in their state or whatever.*

Ms. Balmori: *It is the same with the Park Service.*

Ms. Budow: *But this program is very different from the 50 state quarters in that we are working directly with National Park Service, the Department of Interior and the individual parks and getting their feedback and guidance on designs. And then, as I have mentioned, the governors do provide us with comments. But, again, it is also Secretary Salazar and then the two advisory committees, including the CFA. So it is a different process from the 50 State Quarters.*

Ms. Nelson: *Maybe we need an Aesthetic Czar.*

Mr. Powell: *I think we need to move on in this agenda.*

Ms. Budow: *Thanks for your time.*

Mr. Belle: *Thank you.*

Mr. Luebke: *So we will include some kind of request for some feedback—*

Ms. Balmori: *For a request; yes, please.*

Mr. Luebke: *A report.*

Ms. Balmori: *Yes. Would you?*

Mr. Luebke: *We will have it in writing, so she will hear then.*

Gettysburg

Date: 2011
State: Pennsylvania
Issue: 6 of 56
Mintmarks: P, D & S

Mintage and Pricing

YEAR	MM	MINTAGE	AUCTION	GRADE	PRICE ($)
2011	P	30,800,000	7 Sep 2011	PCGS 70	70
2011	D	30,400,000	7 Sep 2011	PCGS 70	n/a
2011	Collector	15,669			
2011	Unc. Bullion	126,700	3 Jul 2011	NGC Unc	300
2011	S (proof)		13 Mar 2011	PCGS 67	65
2011	S (silver)		7 Sep 2011	PCGS 67	39

Obverse

Bust of George Washington by John Flanagan in 1932 (based on Jean-Antoine Houdon's statue circa 1790). Above Washington's bust reads UNITED STATES OF AMERICA. Beneath his chin reads LIBERTY. Beside his hair braid is the national motto IN GOD WE TRUST. Below his neckline reads QUARTER DOLLAR. On the side of his neckline are John Flanagan's initials JF.

Reverse

Edge: Unmilled; incused with .999 FINE SILVER 5 OUNCE. Reverse at top (L to R) reads GETTYSBURG; bottom (L to R) reads PENNSYLVANIA, 2011, and the motto E PLURIBUS UNUM.

Designed by Joel Iskowitz (AIP Master Designer) and engraved by Phebe Hemphill (U.S. Mint), the reverse features the 72nd Pennsylvania Infantry Monument, which is located on the battle line of the Union Army at Cemetery Ridge.

About the Featured National Park

Gettysburg was the most significant battle between the Union and the Confederate Armies during the Civil War. After his success in Virginia, General Robert E. Lee initiated the Gettsburg Campaign, his second invasion of the North. Intense fighting took place on July 1—3, 1863, in what would be the war's bloodiest battle, claiming about 50,000 lives from both sides.

On the third day, 12,500 Confederate infantry attacked Union positions at Cemetery Ridge. Pickett's Charge, as it is known, failed, and Lee was forced to retreat, dramatically altering the course of the war.

Visitors to Gettysburg National Military Park can see monuments of the battle, and the spot where President Lincoln gave his most famous address.

Grading Hints

The high points of the coin's obverse are prone to contact marks. The field off Washington's nose and behind head curls are prone to contact marks. Reverse: the statue at top, extending, as well as the joint side view will show wear first.

Design finalists for the Gettysburg National
Park quarter.

Notes from the Citizens Coinage Advisory Committee

Meeting notes from 1/26/2010 in Washington D.C.: There was extensive discussion about the coin representing Gettysburg National Military Park in Pennsylvania. Mr. Burdette and several other members suggested that rather than representing a single location or monument, the coin should convey the importance of the Battle of Gettysburg and its place in our nation's history. For Pennsylvania, the committee's recommended design is PA-02, which features the 72nd Pennsylvania Infantry Monument. However, support for this design was limited, with only 12 points out of a maximum possible total of 33. The committee's second most preferred design was PA-04, featuring the Lincoln Speech Memorial, which received three points.

On a motion by Mr. Burdette, seconded by Mr. Scarinci, the committee voted 7-2 to encourage the Mint to consider soliciting additional designs, perhaps more symbolic in nature, to convey the importance of Gettysburg National Military Park.

Recommendation to Secretary Geithner (2/18/2010) said: "For the coin portraying Gettysburg National Military Park in Pennsylvania, several members supported design PA-01, which depicts the 72nd Pennsylvania Infantry Monument. However, several members did not support any of the images presented, and most members would have preferred design concepts related to the Battle of Gettysburg and its vital role in American history. The Committee voted 7-2 to encourage the U. S. Mint to consider soliciting additional designs, perhaps more symbolic in nature, to convey the importance of Gettysburg National Military Park to our Nation."

Notes from the Commission of Fine Arts

Starting with No. 01, this shows the 72nd Pennsylvania Infantry Monument, which is located on the battle line of the Union Army at Cemetery Ridge. It is in the very spot where Confederates broke through the Union Army's battle line during Picket's Charge on the third day of the battle only to be beaten back concluding the battle.

The farms in the background are historic and were there at the time of the fighting. A canon is located in the foreground next to the monument which marks the location where one of the actual artillery batteries fought. Also present is historic Emmitsburg Road to the left, which was used by a portion of the Union Army to reach the battlefield.

Design No. 02 depicts the Eternal Light Peace Memorial dedicated by President Franklin D. Roosevelt on the 75th anniversary of the battle in 1938. The monument bears an eternal flame as well as the inscriptions, "Peace Eternal in Nation United." The monument features an eternal flame and was the inspiration for JFK's grave at Arlington.

No. 03 depicts the Soldiers National Monument. This monument's location is the center of 3,555 graves of Union soldiers who lost their lives in the Battle of Gettysburg. It is emblematic of the sacrifices made by the soldiers for the nation. Today, Soldiers National Cemetery is one of the most honored and visited sites of the park.

The fourth one features the Lincoln Speech Memorial. This monument's location is near the site where President Abraham Lincoln gave his Gettysburg Address in which he honored the Union soldiers who lost their lives and gave his people a clear objective of the war that had to be fought.

And we have a slide showing the four candidate designs for Gettysburg.

Ms. Nelson: *Let me ask you just about the template with the flat bottom. We really all—I think most of us—felt like this flat bottom with the date is awkward and just having a continual circle was superior. But evidently, that flat bottom is standing.*

Ms. Budow: *Yes. We haven't unveiled the designs for 2010 yet. We will be doing that shortly. But as you can see, this is the template that we are proposing to move forward for the series. Yes, this Commission had recommended that it be a full circle.*

Ms. Nelson: *Right.*

Ms. Budow: *We had extensive deliberations and discussions at the highest ranks of the agency, including the chief engraver about the recommendations. It was concluded that this line which we term as "exergue" in medallic art—a very popular device that creates a line or horizon for the central design—would help to orient the viewer to the central design itself and, given the challenges we have with this program going forward and some of these designs which are difficult to show in such a small palette, we think this is a very important feature.*

Ms. Nelson: *So, okay. That has been decided.*

Ms. Budow: *We had very extensive discussions. It was a very important decision moving forward for the program.*

Ms. Nelson: *I feel like the best coin might be 03... Since it is so tiny, a little quarter, it has the least amount of information yet it is very iconic to the cemetery there.*

Mr. Powell: *I agree with that.*

Mr. Rybczynski: *Yes.*

Ms. Plater-Zyberk: *That is the one that does end badly at the bottom. Maybe if you are insisting on the flattening out of the bottom, then instead of that interstices between the base of the sculpture and line above 211, you should just bring down that base so that there is no space. Do you see what I mean?*

Ms. Budow: *Yes.*

Ms. Plater-Zyberk: *Because that just looks like somebody didn't think it* *through. You might also bring the head a little bit further away from the line.*

Ms. Budow: *To sort of clean up the bottom.*

Ms. Plater-Zyberk: *Yes.*

Mr. Powell: *It is the simplest and it is the most iconic of the images.*

Ms. Plater-Zyberk: *I have one question which will affect all the coins, which is the distribution of the words. I think it is obvious that the place wants to be at the top, but paralleling the place and "E Pluribus Unum—" the state and "E Pluribus Unum" on the two sides just seems odd to me. It is almost as if the Latin inscription should always have an honorific place.*

I was going to suggest that maybe that should always be the top and then the location should be on the two sides, the park and the state take the sides. But I may be the only one—

Mr. McKinnell: *No, I agree.*

Mr. Rybczynski: *No, I agree.*

Mr. Powell: *I think it is a well-taken point. But I don't think we are going to get anywhere with it.*

Ms. Budow: *These are being minted as we speak for 2010 with the template that you see here.*

Mr. Powell: *Well, I think it would certainly be worth commenting. I think we all agree with that.*

Mr. Belle: *I agree with that.*

Ms. Nelson: *Put that in the comments. So this is a multi-year—a how-many-year program?*

Ms. Budow: *Twelve years and then there is a possibility of it extending further at the discretion of the secretary.*

Mr. Powell: *Then I would move 03 for the design and underline the comments on the reorganization of the words. Is it just my take, but does the "Unum" come up higher than the P of Pennsylvania?*

Ms. Budow: *Yes. We can check on that.*

Mr. Powell: *It does.*

Ms. Plater-Zyberk: *It is longer.*

Mr. Luebke: *Mr. Chairman, of course, if it is Ohio it will be even more of an issue.*

Mr. Powell: *I know. It just looks like it is kind of lopsided.*

Mr. Belle: *It is.*

Ms. Budow: *Again, one of our challenges and I think some of you see the bookmark showing all the sites that are coming up many years down the* road, some of them are quite long. So, trying to incorporate—

Mr. Powell: *Figure it all out.*

Ms. Budow: *All those inscriptions, yes, was not easy.*

Ms. Plater-Zyberk: *When we make the suggestion, as we are just doing and as we did with the flat bottom, is there any chance of that change happening in a future year? I didn't understand your earlier comment that the Year 2010 is coming up. I didn't get that.*

Ms. Budow: *We introduced the designs for 2010 I think back in October, the candidate designs, and that is when the Commission first introduced the template as well. So the Commission commented on the template.*

As we said, we took that back to the Mint and had extensive discussions about your recommendations.

Ms. Plater-Zyberk: *And that template is for the next 12 years fixed?*

Ms. Budow: *Yes, for the series.*

Ms. Plater-Zyberk: *So we will always see the flat bottom.*

Mr. Powell: *That is the idea.*

Ms. Plater-Zyberk: *And so likewise, the name of the place and the placement of "E Pluribus Unum" will always be this way.*

Ms. Budow: *Correct.*

Ms. Plater-Zyberk: *So we are really only talking about the image from now on.*

Ms. Budow: *Yes.*

Ms. Plater-Zyberk: *Did we really talk about the template as a template? I had no idea that it was fixed forever.*

Mr. Powell: *Yes.*

Mr. Powell: *The Commission made pithy and interesting and appropriate comments, and they were taken into consideration and dispensed with.*

Ms. Budow: *The program may continue after the 12-year period. At that time, we could, again, discuss the template for the future program.*

Glacier

Date: 2011
State: Montana
Issue: 7 of 56
Mintmarks: P, D & S

Mintage and Pricing

YEAR	MM	MINTAGE	AUCTION	GRADE	PRICE ($)
2011	P	30,800,000	30 May 2011	NGC 69	70
2011	D	30,400,000			
2011	Collector	12,574			
2011	Unc. Bullion	126,700	3 Jul 2011	NGC 69	300
2011	S (proof)		1 May 2011	PCGS 67	39
2011	S (silver)		13 Mar 2011	PCGS 70	8

Obverse

Bust of George Washington by John Flanagan in 1932 (based on Jean-Antoine Houdon's statue circa 1790). Above Washington's bust reads UNITED STATES OF AMERICA. Beneath his chin reads LIBERTY. Beside his hair braid is the national motto IN GOD WE TRUST. Below his neckline reads QUARTER DOLLAR. On the side of his neckline are John Flanagan's initials JF.

Reverse

Edge: Unmilled; incused with .999 FINE SILVER 5 OUNCE. Reverse at top (L to R) reads GLACIER; bottom (L to R) reads MONTANA, 2011, and the motto E PLURIBUS UNUM.

Designed by Barbara Fox (AIP Associate Designer) and engraved by Charles L. Vickers (U.S. Mint), the reverse features the rugged majesty of the Northern Rockies with a mountain goat in the foreground.

About the Featured National Park

Glacier National Park's 16,000 square miles covers a vast section of the northern Rocky Mountains. The 130 lakes, 1000-plus species of plant life and 100-plus species of wildlife that include grizzly bears, wolverines, lynx and mountain goats contribute to its remarkable scenic beauty. Known to the Blackfeet as the "Backbone of the World," Glacier was designated the country's 10th national park in 1910.

The park was named for the picturesque alpine terrain and valleys which were born out of the Ice Age some 10,000 years ago. Of the estimated 150 glaciers that existed in the area during the mid-19th century, only about 25 remain today.

Grading Hints

The high points of the coin's obverse are prone to contact marks. The field off Washington's nose and behind head curls are prone to contact marks. Reverse: Mountain goat is focus of high spots: wear concludes, goat's shoulder (right view) picks up bulk of complaint.

Design finalists for the Glacier National Park
quarter.

Notes from the Citizens Coinage Advisory Committee

For the coin portraying Glacier National Park in Montana, the committee unanimously preferred design MT-03, which portrays a mountain goat over the rocky slopes of the park's high country. Members were enthusiastic about the combination of an iconic mountain goat with the grandeur of the mountains and felt this design would translate into a very appealing coin.

Ms. Budow explained that the U.S. Mint works with Superintendents' offices with respect to guidance on appropriate images and source materials for artists.

Committee members rated proposed designs by assigning 0, 1,

2 or 3 points to each, with higher points reflecting more favorable evaluations. With 11 members present and voting, the maximum possible point total is 33.

For the coin portraying Glacier National Park in Montana, the committee unanimously recommended design MT-03, which portrays a mountain goat over the rocky slopes of the park's high country. Mr. Marks spoke passionately in favor of design MT-03, and committee members were quite enthusiastic about the combination of an iconic mountain goat with the grandeur of the mountains. There was a consensus that this design would translate into a very appealing coin.

For Montana, design MT-03 received the maximum possible point total of 33 points. Design MT-01, featuring the north slope of Mount Reynolds, was a distant second, with four points.

Notes from the Commission of Fine Arts

Ms. Budow: *Next is Glacier National Park. Glacier National Park is named for its prominent glacier-carved terrain and remnant glaciers descended from the ice ages of 10,000 years past, glacial forces, ancient seas and geologic faults combine to create spectacular scenery.*

The land also has an established cultural history. By the time the American and European settlers arrived in the late 19th Century, the land was the proud home to many cultures including the Blackfeet, Salish and Kutenai people. It was known to the Native Americans as the Shining Mountains and the Backbone of the World.

Glacier National Park preserves more than a million acres of forest, alpine meadows, lakes, rugged peaks and glacial-carved valleys in the northern Rocky Mountains. It was first established as a national site in 1897 as an effort to preserve the value of the land at a time of great expansion and settlement.

Starting with Design No. 01, this features the north slope of Mt. Reynolds above an alpine meadow with clumps of subalpine fir scattered amid a field of bear grass. So the bear grass are those flowers of the forefront.

No. 02 features Mt. Reynolds with a mountain goat, the largest native mammal found in the alpine sections of the park and, again, bear grass, which is a flower that is most associated with the park.

No. 03 features a classic glacier view. The northeast slope of Mt. Reynolds towers in the distance while a mountain goat clambers over the rocky slopes of Glacier's high country. Again, the trees are the subalpine fir. They pointed out they should look sort of ragged from all the being weather-beaten area. These are the three candidate designs for Glacier.

Ms. Plater-Zyberk: *There is usually already a favorite, isn't there? We refrain from asking for that and we usually tell you what we think. But then—*

Ms. Budow: *We work very closely with the parks. They let us know that all of these designs were historically accurate and appropriate, or emblematic of the park, but did not express a preference.*

Ms. Plater-Zyberk: *They didn't. Okay.*

Mr. Powell: *Well, the simpler is better. No. 01 is simpler. But I am just looking at this—*

Ms. Nelson: *Size.*

Mr. Powell: *Size and since we are left with a template that takes away the... There is not much room on here for a national park.* [Laughter.]

Ms. Budow: *The template is actually quite small, so they give most of the room to the central design element. One thought is that some of these animals, which are very distinctive to selective parks, are a good idea to feature because it helps to distinguish them from other parks down the road.*

Ms. Nelson: *Yes, because they are, like, a mountain and a—*

Ms. Budow: *Exactly. And the bear grass and other flora and fauna that are distinctive to the actual park.*

Ms. Nelson: *I think the design of 03 is fine. I just think it is really hard to get the majesty of all that space on such a little place. But the glacial feature of the mountain seems to work better there, kind of looking more like that.*

Ms. Budow: *And that will be in quite low relief to show the perspective. I thought the chance to see sort of what the new 2010 coins look like, and the template is smaller and the inscriptions are much smaller than the current quarter. So that central design has more room.*

Ms. Plater-Zyberk: *Well, Rusty, I would normally go for the simpler one, but I think actually we could probably reduce most of them landscape and that, in this case, maybe the animal is kind of an appropriate distinction.*

Mr. Powell: *Yes, I think so.*

Ms. Nelson: *Right.*

Mr. Powell: *I think 03.*

Ms. Nelson: *I like 03.*

Ms. Plater-Zyberk: *03.*

Mr. Powell: *Do you want to make a motion for 03?*

Ms. Nelson: *I think 03 is the best of the ones presented here.*
Ms. Plater-Zyberk: *I will second it.*
Mr. Powell: *All in favor.*
[Chorus of ayes.]

Olympic

Date: *2011*
State: *Washington*
Issue: *8 of 56*
Mintmarks: *P, D & S*

Mintage and Pricing

YEAR	MM	MINTAGE	AUCTION	GRADE	PRICE ($)
2011	P	30,400,000	8 May 2011	NGC 69	600
2011	D	30,600,000	22 Nov 2011	NGC 67	21
2011	Collector	5,923	8 May 2011		
2011	Unc. Bullion	84,100	21 Aug 2011		
2011	S (proof)		13 Mar 2011	PCGS 70	70
2011	S (silver)		28 Mar 2011	PCGS 70	90

Obverse

Bust of George Washington by John Flanagan in 1932 (based on Jean-Antoine Houdon's statue circa 1790). Above Washington's bust reads UNITED STATES OF AMERICA. Beneath his chin reads LIBERTY. Beside his hair braid is the national motto IN GOD WE TRUST. Below his neckline reads QUARTER DOLLAR. On the side of his neckline are John Flanagan's initials JF.

Reverse

Edge: Unmilled; incused with .999 FINE SILVER 5 OUNCE. Reverse at top (L to R) reads OLYMPIC; bottom (L to R) reads WASHINGTON, 2011, and the motto E PLURIBUS UNUM.

Designed by Susan Gamble (AIP Master Designer) and engraved by Michael Gaudioso (U.S. Mint), the reverse features an elk crossing the Ho River with Mt. Olympus in the background.

About the Featured National Park

Olympic National Park was established as a national site in 1897 to preserve its diverse wilderness. The nearly one million acres of land was where Native Americans of the Pacific Northwest fished for salmon and hunted for local wildlife in the thousand years prior to the influx of European settlers.

Although none of the paved roads go too far into the park's interior, there are dozens of trails, which allow hikers to explore everything from the coast of the Pacific Ocean to the 8000-foot summit of Mount Olympus. Some of the trails are less than a mile long and can be walked in a few minutes while others might take days.

Grading Hints

The high points of the coin's obverse are prone to contact marks. The field off Washington's nose and behind head curls are prone to contact marks. Reverse: Mountain range beneath peak, to the right of the peak and just underneath, is sufficient to look for wear.

WA-01   WA-02

WA-03   WA-04

Design finalists for the Olympic National Park
quarter.

Notes from the Citizens Coinage Advisory Committee

Notes from recommendation to Treasury Secretary Geithner: For the coin portraying Olympic National Park in Washington, the committee unanimously recommended design WA-01, which features a Roosevelt elk with a view of Mount Olympus in the background. Once again the committee found the combination of the park's wildlife and scenery to be especially compelling.

For Washington, Design WA-01 received the maximum possible total of 33 points. Design WA-02, portraying Sea Stack, received 10 points.

Notes from the Commission of Fine Arts

Design No. 01 depicts a Roosevelt elk, an iconic symbol of Olympic National Park, standing on a gravel river bar with a view of Mt. Olympus in the background. The Ho River is depicted running through the landscape and into the forest. Fallen logs, integral parts of Olympic's forest, can be seen on the ground just to the left of the elk.

Protection of Roosevelt elk was a key reason for the establishment of the park named for President Theodore Roosevelt. Approximately 5,000 Roosevelt elk, the largest herd in the Pacific Northwest, call Olympic National Park their home.

No. 02 features sea stacks or small rocky islands along the coast of Olympic National Park. The 43,000 acres of the park's Pacific coastal strip and offshore islands protect beaches, intertidal areas and rocky tide pools. I actually brought a photograph of this to show because I think it might be easier. This is not exact. This one has more sea stacks in it. This way you can see sort of what the artist was trying to depict with that view.

Then moving on to Design No. 03, this shows a view of a glacier-carved valley with the Ho River flanked by mountains to the north and south.

No. 04 shows a view of the East Fork Quinault River with Mt. Anderson in the background. Mt. Anderson is about 7,330 feet above sea level, not as high as Mt. Olympus.

Ms. Nelson: *I think one thing that is very unique about Olympic National Park is the sea and it having all that shoreline. That might be different than some of the other ones, but I think that is a nicely drawn Roosevelt elk. That might be—I don't know. I am between 01 and 02 thinking, if you want it to be a little different than all the rest of the landscapes, the sea and those rock formations are interesting. But that could be mistaken for—I don't know. I remember it when I went there. I remember those rock stacks.*
Ms. Plater-Zyberk: *I agree with you. It is either 01 or 02. I feel as if we need to give equal time to the animals. But on the other hand, no one else will—would there be other sea-oriented parks?*
Ms. Budow: *There may be some other coastal—*
Ms. Plater-Zyberk: *There will be others.*
Ms. Budow: *—coming down the road. I know the elk is a very important symbol to the park.*

Ms. Plater-Zyberk: *So, then, in that case—*

Ms. Nelson: *I think we will go for 01.*

Mr. Powell: *For the animal one. I am going to go for the elk.*

Mr. Belle: *Yes.*

Mr. Powell: *Do you want to make a motion for the elk?*

Ms. Plater-Zyberk: *I will make a motion for the elk: No. 01.*

Ms. Nelson: *No. 01, all right. Second.*

Mr. Powell: *All in favor.*

[Chorus of ayes.]

Vicksburg

Date: **2011**
State: **Mississippi**
Issue: **9 of 56**
Mintmarks: **P, D & S**

Mintage and Pricing

YEAR	MM	MINTAGE	AUCTION	GRADE	PRICE ($)
2011	P	30,800,000	30 May 2011	NGC 68	70
2011	D	33,400,000	22 Nov 2011	NGC 66	63
2011	Unc. Bullion	33,300			
2011	S (proof)		13 Mar 2011	PCGS 70	85
2011	S (silver)			PCGS 70	65

Obverse

Bust of George Washington by John Flanagan in 1932 (based on Jean-Antoine Houdon's statue circa 1790). Above Washington's bust reads UNITED STATES OF AMERICA. Beneath his chin reads LIBERTY. Beside his hair braid is the national motto IN GOD WE TRUST. Below his neckline reads QUARTER DOLLAR. On the side of his neckline are John Flanagan's initials JF.

Reverse

Edge: Unmilled; incused with .999 FINE SILVER 5 OUNCE. Reverse at top (L to R) reads VICKSBURG; bottom (L to R) reads MISSISSIPPI, 2011, and the motto E PLURIBUS UNUM.

Designed by Thomas Cleveland (AIP Master Designer) and engraved by Joseph Menna (U.S. Mint), the reverse features a Civil War era iron-clad gunboat moving down the Mississippi River.

About the Featured National Park

The Battle of Vicksburg, fought in the summer of 1863 (May 18 to July 4), ended in a brilliant victory for General U.S. Grant and a devastating loss for the Confederacy, effectively splitting its forces in half. The national military park in Mississippi commemorates this historic battle.

The two presidents were both aware of the importance of this city on the Mississippi River. President Lincoln wanted to gain control of the river and divide the South. Likewise, President Jefferson Davis knew it was vital to hold the city for the Confederacy to survive. On hearing the news of Vicksburg's surrender, President Lincoln declared, "The Father of Waters again goes unvexed to the sea."

More than 17,000 Americans (Confederate and Union) died there; the Vicksburg national cemetery is the nation's largest burial site of Civil War Union soldiers and sailors. Of those 17,000 graves, almost 13,000 are unknown.

Grading Hints

The high points of the coin's obverse are prone to contact marks. The field off Washington's nose and behind head curls are prone to contact marks. Reverse: smokestack and steam billowing from the stack, along with front armament, are high points where wear will first be seen.

MS-01

MS-02

MS-03

MS-04

Design finalists for the Vicksburg National
Park quarter.

Notes from the Citizens Coinage Advisory Committee

Meeting notes from 1/26/10: For the coin portraying Vicksburg National Military Park in Mississippi, the committee strongly recommended design MS-02, which carries an image of the USS Cairo on the Mississippi River as it would have appeared during the Civil War. Members felt that this design, in addition to the quality of its composition, has the virtue of showcasing the historical significance of the Navy in the Civil War.

Members also commented on the artistic boldness of the Mississippi African-American Monument on design MS-01, but considered the subject matter of MS-02 to be more historically appropriate.

For Mississippi, Design MS-02 received 27 points out of a maximum possible total of 30. Design MS-01 received 12 points.

Notes from the Commission of Fine Arts

Ms. Budow: *Vicksburg National Military Park commemorates one of the pivotal battles of the Civil War—the campaign, siege and defense of Vicksburg. Surrender on July 4, 1863 followed by the fall of Fort Hudson, Louisiana, split the south giving control of the Mississippi River to the north. These events, coupled with Union victory at Gettysburg, Pennsylvania marked the turning point of the Civil War.*

The battlefield was established as a national military park in 1899. The museum exhibits at the park depict the hardships of civilians and soldiers during the devastating 47-day siege of the city. More than 1,350 monuments and markers including Vicksburg National Cemetery and the restored Union ironclad gunboat, the USS Cairo, marked a 16-mile tour road.

I also brought some images of Vicksburg that might help you. These relate to Design Nos. 03 and 04.

Ms. Plater-Zyberk: *Let me ask you—this, in our notes says, these coins are required to have images on the reverse that are emblematic of a single national site in each state. So, this is a sculpture of the soldiers or is that just the—*

Ms. Budow: *That is a sculpture. And I actually have a copy of that one, too, because that is the top of the sculpture. This is it. Sorry, I forgot to pull this one out. So you can clearly see—*

Ms. Nelson: *That it is a monument.*

Ms. Budow: *Yes, exactly. Sorry.*

Mr. Belle: *It is a reach, isn't it?*

Ms. Nelson: *Yes. I didn't know if it has to be part of the site.*

Ms. Budow: *Yes.*

Ms. Plater-Zyberk: *The base?*

Mr. Powell: *This isn't shown, here.*

Ms. Plater-Zyberk: *In the drawing, it would—*

Ms. Budow: *Actually, the base is shown on the designs that I will walk you through.*

Ms. Nelson: *Oh, the base.*

Ms. Budow: *The base is on the following picture.*

Mr. Powell: *Oh, I see.*

Ms. Budow: *This is showing you what the actual monument looks like. That was part of our struggle, too, between Gettysburg and Vicksburg was also showing monuments and images that are emblematic of that park so you don't confuse the two military parks as well.*

Mr. Powell: *Do you want to put them up?*

Ms. Budow: *No. 01, as a picture I just sent around, features the Mississippi African-African Monument at Vicksburg. The sculpture depicts an African-American Union soldier and a common field hand supporting a wounded African-American Union soldier representing the sacrifice made by Mississippi African-American soldiers during the Civil War.*

The field hand looks behind at the past of slavery while the field soldier gazes toward a future of freedom secured by force of arms on the field of battle. So it is essentially the top of that sculpture.

No. 02 features the USS Cairo, an iron-clad gunboat which was discovered in 1956 in the Yazoo River near the park. In 1972, the U.S. Congress enacted legislation authorizing the National Park Service to accept title to the Cairo and restore the gunboat for display in Vicksburg National Military Park.

The recovery of artifacts from the Cairo revealed a treasure trove of weapons, munitions, naval stores and personal gear of the sailors who served on the boat. The gunboat and its artifacts can now be seen along the tour road at the USS Cairo Museum.

This design shows the USS Cairo on the river as it would have been seen when it served the Union Navy during the Civil War. The USS Cairo had the notoriety of being the first gunboat sunk by an electronically detonated torpedo or mines as they call them today and ushered in a new age of naval warfare.

No. 03. That is the other two photos I sent around, a full image of the monument as well as an image of the portion of the base which the design is based on. This features the Mississippi Memorial, a bronze work that vividly depicts various actions of the Mississippi troops during the siege of Vicksburg. At the monument's front is a statue of Cleo, Muse of History, and a coat of arms of the State of Mississippi.

The flag bearer reflects the courage, bravery and determination of the Mississippi soldiers in the defense of Vicksburg.

No. 04 features the Memorial Arch, which was dedicated at the park in 1920. The dedication inscription reads, "Memorial to the national reunion of Union and Confederate veterans of the Civil War, October 16, 1917."

Mr. McKinnell: *I don't think it would be possible for anybody to understand that either 01 or 03 are the celebration of a park. To me, celebration of an event, but I don't see them in any way celebrating a park.*

Mr. Powell: *I agree with that. I think the idea of this identification, which is opposed—at least the fourth one is specific to the park.*

Ms. Budow: *Or the historical significance of the park is also what the legislation is really intended to promote.*

Ms. Plater-Zyberk: *I think 01 and 03, because they are fragments, you can't tell that they are—unless you know the place, that those are actually monuments and not some kind of storytelling which, of course, a monument is. But I would have taken to 01 much more if it had had a little bit of its base, at least, after looking at the photograph.*

Ms. Nelson: *I think it is the superior coin artistically. But I do think, for putting it to a specific battle and a specific place, that 04 works probably the best. It has a lot going on in there with the foliage and everything.*

Mr. Rybczynski: *I can see 02 or 04, but I can't see this. This is like a photograph pretending to be a coin. I am afraid I feel that way about most of the designs which is why I don't—I haven't voted in support of them.*

If you think of the Gettysburg, the Lincoln Memorial, we don't try to show the grass and the people and the hill. It is just this beautiful view and we recognize it and we know what it is. I could imagine an arch or the boat shown that way. But this way, I think, simply confuses it. It is not a nice coin. It is trying to be everything, trying to be a realistic view.

I think that is a mistake on a coin. I think a coin should symbolize and simplify something so that you see the essence of it, but not the reality of it. So I think I would support 04 but not in this—

Mr. Powell: *I think that is right. I think generally, 04 is an idea that could be further developed.*

Mr. Belle: *Yes.*

Ms. Nelson: *Further stripped of—*

Mr. Powell: *Simplified.*

Ms. Nelson: *Yes, simplified.*

Mr. Belle: *I completely endorse that statement by Witold.*

Mr. Powell: *Then I think, since it is so rare we get a motion from Witold, would you like to make a motion?*

Mr. Rybczynski: *Yes. I would like to support the idea of the design of the theme of the fourth coin but to have a different design that takes away the landscape and doesn't try to show a realistic view but simply an iconic view of this arch.*

Mr. McKinnell: *Second.*

Ms. Nelson: *Second.*

Mr. Belle: *Second.*

Mr. Powell: *This is an historic moment in and of itself. All in favor. [Chorus of ayes.]*

Chickasaw

Date: **2011**
State: **Oklahoma**
Issue: **10 of 56**
Mintmarks: **P, D & S**

Mintage and Pricing

YEAR	MM	MINTAGE	AUCTION	GRADE	PRICE ($)
2011	P	73,800,000			
2011	D	69,400,000			
2011	Collector				
2011	Unc. Bullion	25,900			
2011	S (proof)		13 Mar 2011	PCGS 70	39
2011	S (silver)		13 Mar 2011	PCGS 70	100

Obverse

Bust of George Washington by John Flanagan in 1932 (based on Jean-Antoine Houdon's statue circa 1790). Above Washington's bust reads UNITED STATES OF AMERICA. Beneath his chin reads LIBERTY. Beside his hair braid is the national motto IN GOD WE TRUST. Below his neckline reads QUARTER DOLLAR. On the side of his neckline are John Flanagan's initials JF.

Reverse

Edge: Unmilled; incused with .999 FINE SILVER 5 OUNCE. Reverse at top (L to R) reads CHICKASAW; bottom (L to R) reads OKLAHOMA, 2011, and the motto E PLURIBUS UNUM.

Designed by Donna Weaver (U.S. Mint) and engraved by Jim Licaretz (U.S. Mint), the reverse features the Lincoln Bridge. Built in 1909, the limestone bridge is one of the most beautiful spots at the recreation area.

About the Featured National Park

Established as Sulfur Springs Reservation in 1902, renamed Platte National Park four years later, and combined with Arbuckle Recreation Area in 1976, Chickasaw National Recreation Area is the only national park area in the U.S. established at the request of a Native American tribe.

The park is a dynamic place for outdoor activities like swimming, boating, fishing, picnicking, camping and hiking. As part of the government's agreement with the Chickasaw Nation, the recreation area does not charge admission.

Grading Hints

The high points of the coin's obverse are prone to contact marks. The field off Washington's nose and behind head curls are prone to contact marks. On the reverse, Lincoln Bridge brick stanchion at either end of the bridge show wear as does the top foliage.

OK-01

OK-02

OK-03

Design finalists for the Chickasaw National
Park quarter.

Notes from the Citizens Coinage Advisory Committee

Meeting notes from 1/26/2010: For the coin portraying Chickasaw National Recreation Area in Oklahoma, the committee recommended design OK-01, which features Buffalo Springs amid its stone spillway. Members generally appreciated the perspective and composition of this design, particularly the foreground foliage. However, some members were concerned the human figure would be so small as to be indistinct on the small scale of a coin.

For Oklahoma, design OK-01 received 19 of a possible 30 points. Design OK-02, which shows the Lincoln Bridge, received 11 points.

Notes from the Citizens Coinage Advisory Committee

Meeting notes from 1/26/2010: For the coin portraying Chickasaw National Recreation Area in Oklahoma, the committee recommended design OK-01, which features Buffalo Springs amid its stone spillway. Members generally appreciated the perspective and composition of this design, particularly the foreground foliage. However, some members were concerned the human figure would be so small as to be indistinct on the small scale of a coin.

For Oklahoma, design OK-01 received 19 of a possible 30 points. Design OK-02, which shows the Lincoln Bridge, received 11 points.

Recommendation to the Secretary, 2/18/2010: For the coin portraying Chickasaw National Recreation Area in Oklahoma, the committee preferred design OK-01, which features Buffalo Springs amid its stone spillway. Members generally appreciated the perspective and composition of this design, particularly the foreground foliage. However, some members were concerned that the human figure would be so small as to be indistinct on the small scale of a coin.

Notes from the Commission of Fine Arts

Mr. Powell: *Is there a difference between a national recreation area and a national park hierarchically?*
Ms. Budow: *They are all under the National Park Service.*
Mr. Luebke: *I think the answer is probably yes.*
Ms. Budow: *This is the Buffalo Springs. Here actually are three photographs of the three different designs. So this one features Buffalo Springs, a freshwater seep spring known for its beauty and size. The water of the spring bubbles up into the circular-shaped basin through white sand and spills out over a natural stone spillway with a series of small pools, eventually reaching Travertine Creek.*

Buffalo Springs surfaces to form a rock-bound pool in a restful glade near the eastern end of the park. The spring is situated along the main foot trail, lit through the woodland of the eastern portion of the park.

You will notice that all three designs have a water element. That was a very important feature to the park, to the national recreation area.

No. 02 shows Lincoln Bridge built of limestone and dedicated in 1909 to celebrate the centennial of Abraham Lincoln's birth with flags and ducks overhead. The bridge connects the Flower Park area and City of Sulfur to the mineral springs south of Travertine Creek. After its dedication, the bridge rapidly became a favorite scenic spot within the park. For 100 years the Lincoln Bridge has been a park landmark and a treasured part of the cultural landscape.

And No. 03 depicts Little Niagara, again one of the photographs we provided. The waterfall named after its resemblance to Niagara Falls in New York with a great blue heron flying in the sky. The falls are located in the Travertine Island area of the park.

A 1908 description of the falls noted that "according to photographs and statements, the falls were 15-feet tall and separated at the brink by a jutting rock into two divisions."

Mr. Belle: *May I ask, why did you choose that particular view of the circle rather than the one you just showed us?*

Ms. Budow: *We actually worked with several different versions, and working again in consultation with the park, they felt this was the most appropriate image.*

Mr. Belle: *Appropriate.*

Ms. Budow: *And would execute best in coinage.*

Ms. Plater-Zyberk: *I think the disturbing part of it is the foreground, which is more important than the spring, itself.*

Mr. Powell: *No. 01, you are talking about?*

Mr. Belle: *Yes.*

Ms. Plater-Zyberk: *Yes, No. 01. I would suggest No. 03 with, perhaps, the bird disengaged from the trees so that it has its full silhouette, the way the form of the tail being attached to the background I think might be misleading or disturbing on the coin.*

Mr. Powell: *Other thoughts?*

Mr. McKinnell: *Only a negative one, that No. 01 could be confused with a sort of swimming pool in a rich suburb somewhere.*

Mr. Powell: *I'm with Elizabeth on 03 as a design.*

Mr. McKinnell: *Absolutely.*

Ms. Nelson: *I think it could work.*

Mr. Rybczynski: *I would love to see 03 with just the bird. I would love for somebody at Mint to say, we cannot show landscape on a coin and show an emblem that stands for something because that is what coins have always done. It would be so much stronger, I think, because these are quarters. All this information is not really going to come through, I think.*

Mr. Powell: *That is a heron?*

Ms. Budow: *A great blue heron.*

Mr. Powell: *So you have got a big fight from the Chesapeake Bay and Maryland over the heron isn't generic to—the idea is very good, though.*

Ms. Nelson: *Another thought is the bridge is unique. And just to isolate the form of the bridge and not put everything in it could maybe be an interesting alternative, just the bridge across the coin maybe all by itself. It is unique to the place and it might be an interesting coin. I don't think we have anything we really are very—*

Mr. Belle: *That is what we have said time and time again, the designs are not emblematic.*

Ms. Nelson: *They are very photographic.*

Mr. Powell: *I think you are not getting a sense of community from the—*

Ms. Nelson: *I don't think we have a winner here yet.*

Ms. Budow: *There is no preference or modifications?*

Mr. Powell: *I don't think. I think, clearly, there is no preference on this. I think we would like to see it further developed, the bridge or the... I don't know.*

Ms. Budow: *Or some of the elements simplified?*

Mr. Powell: *Some of the elements—it seems to me the bridge is the strongest graphic direction.*

Ms. Budow: *Great. Thank you for your time.*

Mr. Powell: *Thank you.*

Ms. Nelson: *That is all of them. All right.*

Ms. Budow: *Yes.*

Ms. Nelson: *Thanks for bringing the supplemental pictures, too.*

Mr. Powell: *Yes, that was very helpful.*

El Yunque

Date: 2012
Territory: Puerto Rico
Issue: 11 of 56
Mintmarks: P, D & S

Mintage and Pricing

YEAR	MM	MINTAGE	AUCTION	GRADE	PRICE ($)
2012	P	25,800,000			
2012	D	25,000,000			
2012	S				
2012	Collector				
2012	Unc. Bullion				
2012	S (proof)				
2012	S (silver)				

Obverse

Bust of George Washington by John Flanagan in 1932 (based on Jean-Antoine Houdon's statue circa 1790). Above Washington's bust reads UNITED STATES OF AMERICA. Beneath his chin reads LIBERTY. Beside his hair braid is the national motto IN GOD WE TRUST. Below his neckline reads QUARTER DOLLAR. On the side of his neckline are John Flanagan's initials JF.

Reverse

Edge: Unmilled; incused with .999 FINE SILVER 5 OUNCE. Reverse at top (L to R) reads EL YUNQUE; bottom (L to R) reads PUERTO RICO, 2012, and the motto E PLURIBUS UNUM.

Designed by Gary Whitley (AIP Master Designer) and engraved by Michael Gaudioso (U.S. Mint), the reverse features a Coqui tree frog sitting on a leaf and a Puerto Rican parrot behind an epiphyte plant with tropical flora in the background.

About the Featured National Park

El Yunque is the only tropical rain forest in the National Forest System. Even before Puerto Rico became a U.S. commonwealth, Spain recognized the value of preserving the lush vegetation of the Loquillo Mountains. In 1906, President Theodore Roosevelt followed suit, setting the area aside from development.

El Yunque is home to exotic animals like the endangered Puerto Rican Amazon parrot, which is only found there. Above 2,500 feet, rainfall is nearly constant. Although there are no poisonous snakes or dangerous animals, the wet and windy weather makes camping in the forest a real challenge.

Grading Hints

The high points of the coin's obverse are prone to contact marks. The field off Washington's nose and behind head curls are prone to contact marks. Reverse: Parrots eyes, feathers atop head, branch at center will all take high point wear.

PR-01

PR-02

PR-03

PR-04

PR-05

Design finalists for the El Yunque National
Park quarter.

Notes from the Citizens Coinage Advisory Committee

A public meeting of the Citizens Coinage Advisory Committee was held on Tuesday, October 26, 2010 at U.S. Mint Headquarters in Washington, D.C. For the reverse designs, the Committee recommended design PR-04 for the quarter-dollar coin honoring El Yunque National Park in the Commonwealth of Puerto Rico. The design garnered 12 of a possible 21 points from the Committee.

With seven members present and voting, the maximum possible point total was 21. The Committee's ratings for the El Yunque National Forest designs were:

PR-01: 11
PR-02: 1
PR-03: 4
PR-04: 12
PR-05: 5

Letter to Treasury Secretary Geithner, 11/1/2010: "For the reverse designs to appear on quarter-dollar coins as part of the United States Mint America the Beautiful Quarters® Program, the Committee recommends design four for the quarter-dollar coin honoring El Yunque National Park in the Commonwealth of Puerto Rico. The design garnered 12 of a possible 21 points from the Committee."

Notes from the Commission of Fine Arts

On 10/21/2010, Kaarina Budow introduced John Mercanti, the Mint's chief engraver, who visited from Philadelphia to answer questions regarding artistry and the production process.

A member of the panel asked the chief engraver about design differences between coins and medals. Mr. Mercanti responded that "the design of medals typically has more freedom and abstraction than the design of coins."

Ms. Budow presented the five alternative reverses depicting El Yunque National Forest in Puerto Rico; the subjects included the La Mina waterfall, tropical forest vegetation, a coqui frog, a local parrot, and an observation tower. She said that the depiction of the waterfall in alternatives PR-01 and PR-02 would be stylized with minimal detail and would be polished on the proof coins to convey the appearance of water. Ms. Nelson asked about the legibility of the frog in alternative

PR-01; Ms. Budow confirmed that it would be emphasized through higher relief.

Mr. Belle supported alternatives PR-01 and PR-02 depicting the waterfall. Ms. Nelson agreed, commenting that the polished finish could be interesting; she expressed a preference for alternative PR-02 because it does not include the frog, resulting in a simpler design that is more appropriate for this small coin. She also supported alternative PR-04 due to the profile of the parrot, which is an important animal in the park. Ms. Budow responded that this coin is likely to be the only one in the series with the opportunity to feature a parrot.

Ms. Plater-Zyberk supported alternative PR-04 as a unique depiction of this park, commenting that the waterfall on PR-01 and PR-02 is similar in appearance to waterfalls in other parts of the United States.

Mr. Belle said the frog and parrot are unique elements that should be included. Ms. Plater-Zyberk added the foliage depicted in PR-04 is also unique, and she emphasized each coin should depict distinctive features that will not be repeated on other coins in this series; several Commission members agreed.

A Morgan & Orr coining press, built in 1873, on display at the San Francisco Mint.
Photo courtesy David Shankbone

Starting in 2012, all five national park coins will also be struck as uncirculated circulation strikes at the San Francisco Mint, in addition to the usual circulation strikes at Philadelphia (P) and Denver (D). Production plans call for 1.4 million coins of each design to be produced; though they are of uncirculated quality—and struck at the rate of 70 coins per minute on the Graebener coining press—they will be considered numismatic coins so the total circulating production numbers are not expected to change. Collectors can acquire them in 100 coin bags or 40 coin rolls at face value plus what the mint calls a "nominal premium."

The practical effect is to change the dynamics of existing coin holders. In the Washington quarter series starting in 1932 only the 1937-S (1.652 million), the 1932-D (436,800) and the 1932-S (408,000) have lower mintages.

Ms. Budow responded that the Mint is making an effort to choose distinctive elements in the overall context of the series.

Vice Chairman Nelson summarized the Commission's consensus to recommend alternative PR-04 for El Yunque National Park.

Chaco Culture

Date: 2012
State: New Mexico
Issue: 12 of 56
Mintmarks: P, D & S

Mintage and Pricing

YEAR	MM	MINTAGE	AUCTION	GRADE	PRICE ($)
2012	P	22,000,000			
2012	D	22,000,000			
2012	S				
2012	Collector				
2012	Unc. Bullion				
2012	S (proof)				
2012	S (silver)				

Obverse

Bust of George Washington by John Flanagan in 1932 (based on Jean-Antoine Houdon's statue circa 1790). Above Washington's bust reads UNITED STATES OF AMERICA. Beneath his chin reads LIBERTY. Beside his hair braid is the national motto IN GOD WE TRUST. Below his neckline reads QUARTER DOLLAR. On the side of his neckline are John Flanagan's initials JF.

Reverse

Edge: Unmilled; incused with .999 FINE SILVER 5 OUNCE. Reverse at top (L to R) reads CHACO CULTURE; bottom (L to R) reads NEW MEXICO, 2012, and the motto E PLURIBUS UNUM.

Designed by Donna Weaver (AIP Master Designer) and engraved by Phebe Hemphill (U.S. Mint), the reverse features a view to the west of two elevated kivas that are part of the Chetro Ketl Complex. The design also shows the north wall of Chetro Ketl and the north wall of the canyon. This coin was released April 2, 2012.

About the Featured National Park

In a remote canyon not far from Albuquerque, the Ancient Pueblo peoples built an urban complex that a 1000 years later is still astonishing. Until the 19th century, the 14 "Great Houses" of Chaco Culture National Historical Park were the largest buildings in North America. Its crescent-shaped ceremonial chambers, called kivas, are set to precise solar and lunar alignments. Two hundred miles of straight roads that do not twist or turn with the gulleys and hills in the area connect Chaco Canyon with neighboring settlements. The size and scope of the architectural, engineering and organizational achievements led the United Nations Educational, Scientific and Cultural Organization (UNESCO) to include Chaco Canyon on its list of World Heritage sites.

Grading Hints

The high points of the coin's obverse are prone to contact marks. The field off Washington's nose and behind head curls are prone to contact marks. Reverse: Rocks at upper right, and lining wall will show wear first; then the field.

NM-01

NM-02

NM-03

NM-04

Design finalists for the Chaco Culture
National Park quarter.

Notes from the Citizens Coinage Advisory Committee

A public meeting of the Citizens Coinage Advisory Committee was held on Tuesday, October 26, 2010 at U. S. Mint Headquarters in Washington, D.C. For the reverse designs, the Committee preferred design NM-04 for the quarter-dollar coin honoring Chaco Culture National Historical Park in New Mexico. The design garnered seven of a possible 21 points from the Committee.

With seven members present and voting, the maximum possible point total was 21. The Committee's ratings for the Chaco Culture designs were:

NM-01: 1
NM-02: 3
NM-03: 5
NM-04: 7

Letter to Treasury Secretary Geithner, 11/1/2010: Design four, honoring Chaco Culture National Historical Park in New Mexico, received the highest number of votes among the four candidate designs submitted for review. Having garnered seven of the possible 21 points, the design failed to earn the Committee's recommendation in accordance with the Committee's policy that a design must achieve more than 50 percent of the possible points to qualify for a recommendation.

Notes from the Commission of Fine Arts

Ms. Budow noted the park was originally established as Chaco Canyon National Monument in 1907, and, as the extent and sophistication of the Chaco civilization became better understood, was expanded and redesignated as an historical park in 1980. The civilization flourished between 850 and 1200 A.D. and extended across a 40,000-square-mile area. The park protects the distinctive massive masonry ruins that survive, with complex architecture and exceptional planning, engineering and execution. Ms. Budow presented the four alternative reverses depicting Chaco structures and a prominent butte in the park.

Ms. Nelson acknowledged the challenge of depicting this park on a coin. She supported alternative NM-04, commenting that it captures the vastness of the natural setting as well as the human contribution of a Chaco structure. Several Commission members supported this preference, with no recommendation for modifications. Vice Chairman Nelson summarized the Commission's consensus to recommend alternative NM-04 for Chaco Culture National Historical Park.

Acadia

Date: 2012
State: Maine
Issue: 13 of 56
Mintmarks: P, D & S

Mintage and Pricing

YEAR	MM	MINTAGE	AUCTION	GRADE	PRICE ($)
2012	P				
2012	D				
2012	S				
2012	Collector				
2012	Unc. Bullion	27,000			
2012	S (proof)	1,105,530			
2012	S (silver)	635,907			

Obverse

Bust of George Washington by John Flanagan in 1932 (based on Jean-Antoine Houdon's statue circa 1790). Above Washington's bust reads UNITED STATES OF AMERICA. Beneath his chin reads LIBERTY. Beside his hair braid is the national motto IN GOD WE TRUST. Below his neckline reads QUARTER DOLLAR. On the side of his neckline are John Flanagan's initials JF.

Reverse

Edge: Unmilled; incused with .999 FINE SILVER 5 OUNCE. Reverse at top (L to R) reads ACADIA; bottom (L to R) reads MAINE, 2012, and the motto E PLURIBUS UNUM.

Designed and engraved by Joseph Menna (U.S. Mint), the reverse features Bass Harbor Head Lighthouse and Acadia's rough coastline.

About the Featured National Park

The first national park east of the Mississippi River, Acadia National Park in Bar Harbor, Maine is primarily an island made up of more than 47,000 acres of rocky, mountainous terrain. In addition to most of Mount Desert Island, the park extends to most of Isle au Haut, parts of Baker Island, and a section of Schoodic Peninsula on the mainland. There are 120 miles of trails—some very easy to walk while others are so steep hikers must use ladders and iron rungs. Wildlife in the park includes moose, beaver, porcupine, muskrats, bobcats, foxes and black bears. Acadia National Park, originally called Lafayette National Park, celebrates its centennial in 2016.

Grading Hints

The high points of the coin's obverse are prone to contact marks. The field off Washington's nose and behind head curls are prone to contact marks. Reverse: Rocks at right, lighthouse will show wear first.

ME-01

ME-02

ME-03

ME-04

ME-05

Design finalists for the Acadia National Park
quarter.

Notes from the Citizens Coinage Advisory Committee

Letter to Secretary Geithner, 11/1/2010: For the quarter-dollar coin honoring Acadia National Park in Maine, the Committee recommended design ME-04, showing a lighthouse. The design garnered 14 of the possible 21 points. Kaarina Budow of the U.S. Mint presented the proposed 2012 quarter-dollar coin reverse designs honoring Acadia National Park in Maine to be issued as part of the U.S. Mint America the Beautiful Quarters Program.

After discussions concerning the designs, Committee members rated proposed designs by assigning zero, one, two, or three points to each, with higher points reflecting more favorable evaluations. With seven members present and voting, the maximum possible point total was 21. The Committee's ratings for the Acadia National Park designs were:

ME-01: 1
ME-02: 1
ME-03: 11
ME-04: 14
ME-05: 0

Notes from the Commission of Fine Arts

Kaarina Budow of the U.S. Mint presented the proposed 2012 quarter-dollar coin reverse designs honoring Acadia National Park in Maine to be issued as part of the U.S. Mint America the Beautiful Quarters Program.

Ms. Budow presented the five alternative reverses for Acadia National Park, depicting various combinations of scenic beauty, an historic gatehouse along a carriage road, and the Bass Harbor Head Lighthouse.

Ms. Nelson commented that the strongest alternative is ME-03, depicting the lighthouse atop a cliff; she noted the rocky coast is emblematic of Maine, and the lighthouse is an iconic feature of the park.

Mr. McKinnell and Mr. Rybczynski supported this recommendation. Ms. Plater-Zyberk suggested the composition be shifted to the right so that more of the ocean could be depicted on the left part of the coin; she added the submitted design gives excessive emphasis to the rocks. Mr. Belle agreed, adding the tree at the upper right edge of the design could be omitted.

Ms. Plater-Zyberk commented that ME-02, depicting the rocky coast with ocean spray behind, is an iconic view that may not be legible on a coin. Ms. Budow noted that a lighthouse was included in the previous series of 50 state quarters, and officials of the park suggested another design feature could be preferable. Ms. Plater-Zyberk acknowledged this concern but said that the ocean spray in ME-02 is too problematic in its rendering, resulting in her support for ME-03.

Vice Chairman Nelson summarized the Commission's consensus to recommend alternative ME-03 for Acadia National Park, with the request to shift the composition in order to provide more space for the depiction of the ocean. Ms. Plater-Zyberk added this shift would also move the lighthouse tower away from the center of the coin, appropriately reducing its importance in the composition.

Hawai'i Volcanoes

Date: *2012*
State: *Hawaii*
Issue: *14 of 56*
Mintmarks: *P, D & S*

Mintage and Pricing

YEAR	MM	MINTAGE	AUCTION	GRADE	PRICE ($)
2012	P				
2012	D				
2012	S				
2012	Collector				
2012	Unc. Bullion				
2012	S (proof)				
2012	S (silver)				

Obverse

Bust of George Washington by John Flanagan in 1932 (based on Jean-Antoine Houdon's statue circa 1790). Above Washington's bust reads UNITED STATES OF AMERICA. Beneath his chin reads LIBERTY. Beside his hair braid is the national motto IN GOD WE TRUST. Below his neckline reads QUARTER DOLLAR. On the side of his neckline are John Flanagan's initials JF.

Reverse

Edge: Unmilled; incused with .999 FINE SILVER 5 OUNCE. Reverse at top (L to R) reads HAWAII VOLCANOES; bottom (L to R) reads HAWAII, 2012, and the motto E PLURIBUS UNUM.

Designed and engraved by Charles L. Vickers (U.S. Mint), the reverse features an eruption on the east rift of Kilauea Volcano.

About the Featured National Park

Hawaii Volcanoes National Park, on the Big Island, showcases two of Hawaii's five volcanoes. The main road around Kilauea, one of the world's most active volcanoes, is closed periodically due to lava flows, and visitors are warned of vents emitting dangerous gases. Mauna Loa, the world's largest volcano rises 13,600 feet above sea level, but measured from the sea floor is 56,000 feet high. The dramatic altitude difference means the ecosystems at the base of Mauna Loa are completely different from the summit. It can easily be sunny at sea level and have a raging snow storm at the peak. The park was established in 1916.

Grading Hints

The high points of the coin's obverse are prone to contact marks. The field off Washington's nose and behind head curls are prone to contact marks. Reverse: Volcanic ash and lava will show wear first.

HI-01

HI-02

HI-03

HI-04

HI-05

Design finalists for the Hawaii Volcanoes
National Park quarter.

Notes from the Citizens Coinage Advisory Committee

Kaarina Budow of the U.S. Mint presented proposed 2012 quarter-dollar coin reverse designs honoring Hawaii Volcanoes National Park in Hawaii to be issued as part of the U.S. Mint America the Beautiful Quarters Program.

After discussions concerning the designs, Committee members rated proposed designs by assigning zero, one, two or three points to each, with higher points reflecting more favorable evaluations. With seven members present and voting, the maximum possible point total was 21. The Committee's ratings for the Hawaii Volcanoes National Park designs were:

HI-01: 1
HI-02: 1
HI-03: 1
HI-04: 15
HI-05: 1

Letter to Secretary Geithner, 11/1/2010: Design HI-04, honoring the Hawaii Volcanoes National Park, earned the Committee's recommendation with 15 of the possible 21 points. Members commented that they were intrigued with the modern style of the design. Other designs for this quarter-dollar coin received very little support from the Committee.

Notes from the Commission of Fine Arts

On 10/21/2010, Ms. Budow described the Hawaii Volcanoes National Park, which extends from sea level to an elevation of nearly 14,000 feet and encompasses two active volcanoes as well as archaeological sites, in terms of its significance to native Hawaiian culture. She presented the five alternative reverses with depictions of the volcanoes, lava flows and native Hawaiian dances, noting the stylized depictions of the lava flow would be polished on the proof coins to suggest a liquid state.

Ms. Nelson asked for clarification of the surface detailing in alternative HI-04, depicting an exploding volcano. John Mercanti, the Mint's chief engraver, responded that the background would be textured, the mountain would be modeled, and the lava flow would be polished; he described the composition as very stylistic. Ms. Nelson asked about the relief treatment, and Mr. Mercanti confirmed the mountain would be raised above the background.

Ms. Nelson recommended HI-04, commenting this single image of a volcano would be the most compelling composition for the small coin, resulting in a unique and interesting design. Several Commission members agreed. Mr. McKinnell added this alternative is perhaps the first presented to the Commission in recent years that has the stylization appropriate to coin design, rather than the more typical effort to convey a narrative. Vice Chairman Nelson summarized the consensus of the Commission, recommending HI-04 for Hawaii Volcanoes National Park.

Denali

Date: 2012
State: Alaska
Issue: 15 of 56
Mintmarks: P, D & S

Mintage and Pricing

YEAR	MM	MINTAGE	AUCTION	GRADE	PRICE ($)
2012	P				
2012	D				
2012	S				
2012	Collector				
2012	Unc. Bullion				
2012	S (proof)				
2012	S (silver)				

Obverse

Bust of George Washington by John Flanagan in 1932 (based on Jean-Antoine Houdon's statue circa 1790). Above Washington's bust reads UNITED STATES OF AMERICA. Beneath his chin reads LIBERTY. Beside his hair braid is the national motto IN GOD WE TRUST. Below his neckline reads QUARTER DOLLAR. On the side of his neckline are John Flanagan's initials JF.

Reverse

Edge: Unmilled; incused with .999 FINE SILVER 5 OUNCE. Reverse at top (L to R) reads DENALI; bottom (L to R) reads ALASKA, 2012, and the motto E PLURIBUS UNUM.

Designed by Susan Gamble (AIP Master Designer) and engraved by Jim Licaretz (U.S. Mint), the reverse features a Dall sheep with Mount McKinley rising in the background.

About the Featured National Park

Denali National Park and Preserve is comprised of over 6 million acres of federal land, about the size of the state of Maryland. Mountain climbers from around the world come to the park for the challenge of Mount McKinley, the tallest mountain in North America at 20,300 feet above sea level. Wildlife includes grizzly bears, Dall sheep, caribou and gray wolves. Snow can come anywhere in Denali at any time of the year. While average summer temperatures are relatively balmy, ranging from 33 to 75 degrees Fahrenheit, winters are not meant for family visits, with temperatures falling as low as 40-below zero.

Grading Hints

The high points of the coin's obverse are prone to contact marks. The field off Washington's nose and behind head curls are prone to contact marks. Reverse: The ram and the mountain (top) is likely high point to show wear first.

AK-01

AK-02

AK-03

AK-04

AK-05

Design finalists for the Denali National Park
quarter.

Notes from the Citizens Coinage Advisory Committee

After discussions concerning the designs, Committee members rated proposed designs by assigning zero, one, two, or three points to each, with higher points reflecting more favorable evaluations. With seven members present and voting, the maximum possible point total was 21. The Committee's ratings for the Denali National Park designs were:

AK-01: 5
AK-02: 16
AK-03: 3
AK-04: 1
AK-05: 6

Letter to Secretary Geithner, 11-1-2010: Finally, the Committee recommended design AK-02 for the quarter-dollar coin honoring Denali National Park in Alaska. The design received 16 of 21 possible points. A motion was made to recommend that consideration be given to enlarging the Dall sheep appearing on the Committee's recommended design, AK-02. The motion was approved on a vote of 5-2.

Notes from the Commission of Fine Arts

Ms. Budow said the park, initially established as Mount McKinley National Park, was the first to be created as a wildlife refuge; the mountain itself was not included in the park until its boundaries were expanded in 1980. She presented the five alternative reverses depicting the mountain, a Dall sheep and a hiker.

Ms. Plater-Zyberk recommended AK-02.

Ms. Nelson questioned the composition of AK-02, with both the mountain and the sheep toward the center of the coin, and instead supported AK-05 due to the high quality of the drawing. She said the composition of AK-01 is more dynamic, but the sheep may be too small for the scale of the coin. She added that the background depiction of the mountain in the alternatives should be de-emphasized because many coins will depict mountains, which will be difficult for the public to distinguish.

Mr. Rybczynski also supported AK-02, because the sheep is largest in this alternative; he commented on the simplicity of this design and suggested that the sheep could be shown even larger. Mr. Belle, too, supported AK-02.

Ms. Budow responded that the mountain would be rendered in low relief, providing greater emphasis to the sheep; Ms. Nelson and Mr. McKinnell supported this design effect as helping to strengthen the composition. Ms. Budow agreed to convey the request to the artist to de-emphasize the mountain by using low relief.

Vice Chairman Nelson summarized the consensus of the Commission to recommend AK-02 for Denali National Park, with the suggestion to enlarge the depiction of the Dall sheep.

White Mountain

Date: *2013*
State: *New Hampshire*
Issue: *16 of 56*
Mintmarks: *P, D & S*

Design recommended by the Commission of Fine Arts.

Mintage and Pricing

YEAR	MM	MINTAGE	AUCTION	GRADE	PRICE ($)
2013	P				
2013	D				
2013	S				
2013	Collector				
2013	Unc. Bullion				
2013	S (proof)				
2013	S (silver)				

Obverse

Bust of George Washington by John Flanagan in 1932 (based on Jean-Antoine Houdon's statue circa 1790). Above Washington's bust reads UNITED STATES OF AMERICA. Beneath his chin reads LIBERTY. Beside his hair braid is the national motto IN GOD WE TRUST. Below his neckline reads QUARTER DOLLAR. On the side of his neckline are John Flanagan's initials JF.

Reverse

Edge: Unmilled; incused with .999 FINE SILVER 5 OUNCE. Reverse at top (L to R) reads WHITE MOUNTAIN; bottom (L to R) reads NEW HAMPSHIRE, 2013, and the motto E PLURIBUS UNUM.

The final rendition for the reverse has not yet been chosen.

About the Featured National Park

White Mountain National Forest, located primarily in New Hampshire but partly in Maine, is 777,496 acres of the most beautiful birches, sugar maples and American beeches, especially in autumn when their leaves explode with vibrant colors. Early settlers tried to clear away the land for farming, but when the soil proved largely unproductive commercial loggers took over the area. Today, in addition to limited logging, the park is popular for its snow skiing, hiking and mountain biking.

White Mountain National Forest is the largest area of publicly owned land in the six New England states. It was established by Presidential proclamation on May 16, 1918 by Woodrow Wilson.

Grading Hints

The high points of the coin's obverse are prone to contact marks. The field off Washington's nose and behind head curls are prone to contact marks. Reverse: Will depend upon the final design.

Notes from the Commission of Fine Arts

In the minutes, Ms. Balmori supported alternative NH-01, depicting Mount Washington framed by white birch trees, as a simple design that would work well on a coin. She said NH-05 could also be successful with a larger rendition of the moose and a simple mountain profile in the background, without the additional design elements that are shown. Mr. Powell and Mr. McKinnell joined in supporting NH-01. Following a motion by Mr. Powell with second by Ms. Balmori, the Commission recommended NH-01 for White Mountain National Forest.

Letter of Oct. 27, 2011 from Thomas E. Luebke, FAIA, Secretary, Commission on Fine Arts to U.S. Mint Deputy Director Richard A. Peterson: "In its meeting of 20 October, the Commission of Fine Arts reviewed the proposed reverse designs for the five America the Beautiful Quarters for issue in 2013. The Commission reiterated its previous concern regarding excessive design complexity for the small size of the quarter-dollar coin. The Commission's specific recommendations were as follows: White Mountain National Forest (New Hampshire), the Commission recommended alternative NH-01 due to the simplicity of the composition."

Perry's Victory

Date: **2013**
State: **Ohio**
Issue: **17 of 56**
Mintmarks: **P, D & S**

Two design proposals for Perry's Victory contain flags of a foreign nation, which would be a first for U.S. circulating coinage.

Mintage and Pricing

YEAR	MM	MINTAGE	AUCTION	GRADE	PRICE ($)
2013	P				
2013	D				
2013	S				
2013	Collector				
2013	Unc. Bullion				
2013	S (proof)				
2013	S (silver)				

Obverse

Bust of George Washington by John Flanagan in 1932 (based on Jean-Antoine Houdon's statue circa 1790). Above Washington's bust reads UNITED STATES OF AMERICA. Beneath his chin reads LIBERTY. Beside his hair braid is the national motto IN GOD WE TRUST. Below his neckline reads QUARTER DOLLAR. On the side of his neckline are John Flanagan's initials JF.

Reverse

Edge: Unmilled; incused with .999 FINE SILVER 5 OUNCE. Reverse at top (L to R) reads PERRY'S VICTORY; bottom (L to R) reads OHIO, 2013, and the motto E PLURIBUS UNUM.

The final rendition for the reverse has not yet been chosen.

About the Featured National Park

At dawn on the morning of September 10, 1813, a lookout spotted six vessels to the northwest of Rattlesnake Island in Lake Erie, then under British control. American Commodore Oliver Hazard Perry made preparations to sail forth and attack the British.

Just before the engagement Perry hoisted his personal battle flag inscribed DON'T GIVE UP THE SHIP. Perry fought tenaciously in this fierce naval battle off the coast of Ohio. Perry's own vessel, the USS *Lawrence*, was nearly sunk by the British, and he transferred his personal standard to the *Niagra*. Six vessels of Great Britain's Royal Navy were captured. Perry wrote to Major General William Henry Harrison (who would later become president), "We have met the enemy and they are ours. Two ships, two brigs, one schooner and one sloop. Yours with great respect and esteem."

Perry's Victory and International Peace Memorial was established to honor those who fought in the Battle of Lake Erie during the War of 1812 and to celebrate the lasting peace between Britain, Canada and the United States. The Memorial, a Doric column that rises 352-feet over Lake Erie, is currently closed to visitors, but there are a variety of activities and ranger programs at the Visitor Center.

Grading Hints

The high points of the coin's obverse are prone to contact marks. The field off Washington's nose and behind head curls are prone to contact marks. Reverse: Will depend upon the final design.

OH-01   OH-02

OH-03

Design finalists for the Perry's Victory
National Park quarter.

Notes from the Citizens Coinage Advisory Committee

The Citizens Coinage Advisory Committee voted on Nov. 29, 2011 to reject all three proposed designs proposed by the U.S. Mint for the International Peace Memorial. It was unable to suggest a way to revise one design (which featured a statue of Commodore Oliver Perry) and the memorial marking the Battle of Lake Erie during the War of 1812. On the first go round, the proposal fell four shy of the 11 points needed for a favorable recommendation to the Treasury secretary. They voted four to three to reject all designs for the Ohio coin, calling them seriously flawed. Member Donald Scarinci said, "There is nothing artistic here. Nobody could think anything is good here."

Notes from the Commission of Fine Arts

Cynthia Meals Vitelli of the Mint presented the three alternative reverses depicting the memorial to the Battle of Lake Erie in the War of 1812; the memorial is also a symbol of the longstanding peace between Great Britain, Canada and the United States, and the 352–foot–high granite column is a dominant feature of the islands in the western part of Lake Erie.

Ms. Balmori and Ms. Fernández commented that all three alternatives are problematic as designs for a coin. Ms. Fernández said the row of three flags in OH-02 has the effect of flattening the image, undermining the perception of the column in the background as a rounded three-dimensional object. She added that OH-03 has an excess of negative space and its depiction of the three flags is not readily legible, while OH-01 has a confusing combination of foreground and background scales. She suggested the Commission request a redesign of the alternatives for this coin; Ms. Balmori agreed, and Chairman Powell summarized this response as the consensus of the Commission.

Letter of Oct. 27, 2011 from Thomas E. Luebke, FAIA, Secretary, Commission on Fine Arts to U.S. Mint Deputy Director Richard A. Peterson: "The Commission did not recommend any of the three submitted alternatives, citing the compositional problems in each of them. The complex layering of design elements in OH-01 would be incomprehensible at the scale of the coin. The row of flags in OH-02 has the effect of flattening the perspective view, and the large area of negative space in OH-03 is unbalanced and excessive."

Great Basin

Date: 2013
State: Nevada
Issue: 18 of 56
Mintmarks: P, D & S

Design recommended by the Commission of Fine Arts.

Mintage and Pricing

YEAR	MM	MINTAGE	AUCTION	GRADE	PRICE ($)
2013	P				
2013	D				
2013	S				
2013	Collector				
2013	Unc. Bullion				
2013	S (proof)				
2013	S (silver)				

Obverse

Bust of George Washington by John Flanagan in 1932 (based on Jean-Antoine Houdon's statue circa 1790). Above Washington's bust reads UNITED STATES OF AMERICA. Beneath his chin reads LIBERTY. Beside his hair braid is the national motto IN GOD WE TRUST. Below his neckline reads QUARTER DOLLAR. On the side of his neckline are John Flanagan's initials JF.

Reverse

Edge: Unmilled; incused with .999 FINE SILVER 5 OUNCE. Reverse at top (L to R) reads GREAT BASIN; bottom (L to R) reads NEVADA, 2013, and the motto E PLURIBUS UNUM.

The final rendition for the reverse has not yet been chosen.

About the Featured National Park

Formerly called Lehman Caves National Monument, Great Basin National Park changed its name to highlight the other natural wonders in this remote section of northern Nevada. Because of the lack of any major city nearby, there is a blanket of darkness that coupled with the high elevations, which range from 6,500 to 12,000 feet, the park offers some of the best star gazing in the country.

Its 5,000-year-old bristlecone pines are among the oldest known living organisms. Of Great Basin's 40 caves, eight are made available to experienced spelunkers.

Grading Hints

The high points of the coin's obverse are prone to contact marks. The field off Washington's nose and behind head curls are prone to contact marks. Reverse: Will depend upon the final design.

NV-01   NV-02

NV-03   NV-04

Design finalists for the Great Basin National
Park quarter.

Notes from the Commission of Fine Arts

Cynthia Meals Vitelli presented the four alternative reverses depicting Great Basin National Park in Nevada, an expansive area located within the overall Great Basin that extends from California to Utah. The subjects include the distinctive terrain, pine trees, mountains and bighorn sheep. Ms. Balmori offered support for NV-01 because of its emphasis on a single design feature that will be legible at the scale of the coin, while the other alternatives have an excess of elements. Mr. McKinnell agreed. Upon a motion by Ms. Balmori with second by Ms. Fernández, the Commission recommended NV-01 for Great Basin National Park.

Letter of Oct. 27, 2011 from Thomas E. Luebke, FAIA, Secretary, Commission on Fine Arts to U.S. Mint Deputy Director Richard A. Peterson: "The Commission recommended NV-01, citing the legibility of the composition with a single major design element."

Fort McHenry

Date: 2013
State: Maryland
Issue: 19 of 56
Mintmarks: P, D & S

Committee members were unable to recommend a design preference, citing the alternatives, like MD-04 above, as focusing on the soldiers rather than the fort.

Mintage and Pricing

YEAR	MM	MINTAGE	AUCTION	GRADE	PRICE ($)
2013	P				
2013	D				
2013	S				
2013	Collector				
2013	Unc. Bullion				
2013	S (proof)				
2013	S (silver)				

Obverse

Bust of George Washington by John Flanagan in 1932 (based on Jean-Antoine Houdon's statue circa 1790). Above Washington's bust reads UNITED STATES OF AMERICA. Beneath his chin reads LIBERTY. Beside his hair braid is the national motto IN GOD WE TRUST. Below his neckline reads QUARTER DOLLAR. On the side of his neckline are John Flanagan's initials JF.

Reverse

Edge: Unmilled; incused with .999 FINE SILVER 5 OUNCE. Reverse at top (L to R) reads FORT McHENRY; bottom (L to R) reads MARYLAND, 2013, and the motto E PLURIBUS UNUM.

The final rendition for the reverse has not yet been chosen.

About the Featured National Park

In the midst of the War of 1812, a young lawyer named Francis Scott Key was negotiating a prison exchange on the British flagship HMS *Tonnant* when Fort McHenry came under a vicious attack. At dawn, Key reported to the prisoners below deck that the American flag still flew.

The experience was the inspiration from which Key wrote the immortal lines that would become the lyrics to the country's national anthem, "The Star Spangled Banner."

The fort, named after George Washington's Secretary of War James McHenry, has the shape of a five-pointed star, which meant its 43 acres could be manned with only five lookouts.

Grading Hints

The high points of the coin's obverse are prone to contact marks. The field off Washington's nose and behind head curls are prone to contact marks. Reverse: Will depend upon the final design.

MD-01   MD-02

MD-03   MD-04

Design finalists for the Fort McHenry
National Park quarter.

Notes from the Citizens Coinage Advisory Committee

The Citizens Advisory Committee essentially dealt with Fort McHenry twice, once with the America the Beautiful issue, the second time with the 2012 commemorative coins authorized by Congress. Their comments on the commemorative coin (not intended for circulation) express some of the difficulty the Commission of Fine Arts appears to have also felt.

The Committee dedicated extensive consideration to recommending obverse and reverse designs for the 2012 Star Spangled Banner Commemorative Coin Program that would complement each other, produce well for the relative sizes of the $1 silver coin and the

$5 gold coin, and give appropriate deference to the subject matter of "The Star Spangled Banner." To those ends, the Committee reviewed 16 obverse candidate designs and 17 reverse designs for both the silver and gold coins, and identified designs for each coin, respectively.

Notes from the Commission of Fine Arts

Cynthia Meals Vitelli presented the four alternative reverses depicting star-shaped Fort McHenry, notable for its role in the War of 1812 when it served as inspiration for "The Star-Spangled Banner."

The alternatives depict varying configurations of soldiers in front of the fort with the historic flag flying above. Ms. Balmori commented the alternatives include too many design elements, and the human figures are awkwardly drawn. Ms. Fernández suggested the Mint develop new alternatives.

Mr. Powell suggested an elevated view of the fort to illustrate its well-known and elegant shape; Ms. Balmori agreed. Ms. Vitelli responded that an elevated view was considered for the recently submitted commemorative coin design depicting Fort McHenry and could also be considered for the circulating quarter. Mr. Powell added that the submitted alternatives appear to treat the soldiers rather than the fort as the subject; Ms. Plater-Zyberk agreed the background image is not clearly legible as a fort and that an elevated view would be preferable.

Letter of Oct. 27, 2011 from Thomas E. Luebke, FAIA, Secretary, Commission on Fine Arts to U.S. Mint Deputy Director Richard A. Peterson: "The Commission did not recommend any of the submitted alternatives, criticizing the crowded compositions and excessive emphasis on the human figures rather than the fort itself. The Commission suggested consideration of an elevated or plan view of Fort McHenry that would convey its iconic five-sided shape."

Mount Rushmore

Date: **2013**
State: **South Dakota**
Issue: **20 of 56**
Mintmarks: **P, D & S**

Design recommended by the Commission of Fine Arts.

Mintage and Pricing

YEAR	MM	MINTAGE	AUCTION	GRADE	PRICE ($)
2013	P				
2013	D				
2013	S				
2013	Collector				
2013	Unc. Bullion				
2013	S (proof)				
2013	S (silver)				

Obverse

Bust of George Washington by John Flanagan in 1932 (based on Jean-Antoine Houdon's statue circa 1790). Above Washington's bust reads UNITED STATES OF AMERICA. Beneath his chin reads LIBERTY. Beside his hair braid is the national motto IN GOD WE TRUST. Below his neckline reads QUARTER DOLLAR. On the side of his neckline are John Flanagan's initials JF.

Reverse

Edge: Unmilled; incused with .999 FINE SILVER 5 OUNCE. Reverse at top (L to R) reads MOUNT RUSHMORE; bottom (L to R) reads SOUTH DAKOTA, 2013, and the motto E PLURIBUS UNUM.

The final rendition for the reverse has not yet been chosen.

About the Featured National Park

Carved into the face of Mount Rushmore, in the Black Hills near Keystone, South Dakota, is the colossal sculpture by Danish-American Gutzon Borglum and his son, Lincoln, that features the heads of George Washington, Thomas Jefferson, Theodore Roosevelt and Abraham Lincoln.

Borglum said of the iconic monument, "We are not here trying to carve an epic, portray a moonlight scene, or write a sonnet; We are cool-headedly, clear-mindedly setting down a few crucial, epochal facts regarding the accomplishments of the Old World radicals who shook the shackles of oppression from their light feet and fled despotism to people a continent; who built an empire and rewrote the philosophy of freedom and compelled the world to accept a wiser, happier form of government."

Work began in 1927, and the faces were completed between 1934 and 1939.

Grading Hints

The high points of the coin's obverse are prone to contact marks. The field off Washington's nose and behind head curls are prone to contact marks. Reverse: Will depend upon the final design.

SD-01   SD-02

SD-03   SD-04

Design finalists for the Mount Rushmore
National Park quarter.

Notes from the Commission of Fine Arts

Cynthia Meals Vitelli of the U.S. Mint presented design submissions of the four alternative reverses depicting the presidential portraits carved into the granite of Mount Rushmore. She noted the Mint had previously issued several coins depicting Mount Rushmore, including a commemorative coin in the 1990s and a recent state quarter. The current proposal is, therefore, intended to provide a different type of design approach, including an aerial perspective view or depictions of the sculpting process.

Ms. Balmori offered support for SD-03, saying it is a strong design; Mr. Powell commented on the greatly contrasting scale of the human stonecarvers against the large faces of the sculpture. Ms. Vitelli noted the coin sculpting process could enhance the level of detail for the scene. Mr. Powell said SD-03 would be acceptable if the coin sculpting process is executed well.

Ms. Plater–Zyberk thought SD-04 would confuse the public due to the depiction of maquettes that differ substantially from the familiarly executed sculpture; Ms. Balmori concurred, adding the renderings of the figures in SD-04 are unsatisfactory.

Mr. McKinnell supported SD-02 and SD-03; Mr. Powell commented that SD-03 is the simpler design. Upon a motion by Ms. Balmori, the Commission recommended SD-03 for Mount Rushmore.

Letter of Oct. 27, 2011 from Thomas E. Luebke, FAIA, Secretary, Commission on Fine Arts to U.S. Mint Deputy Director Richard A. Peterson: The Commission recommended SD-03 as the strongest design."

Great Smoky Mountains

Date: 2014
State: Tennessee
Issue: 21 of 56
Mintmarks: P, D & S

Great Smoky Mountains National Park headquarters, near Gaitlinburg, Tennessee. *Photo by Brian Stansberry*

About the Featured National Park

Nine million people come to Great Smoky Mountains National Park each year, making it America's most visited national park. Its rugged mountain scenery is home to 1,500 black bears, 50 different species of trout, and peregrine falcons to name but a few of the diverse wildlife there.

Congress authorized the park in 1926, but left it crucially unfunded. John D. Rockefeller eventually contributed $5 million, the U.S. government $2 million, and in 1940 President Franklin D. Roosevelt dedicated the 816 square mile park, one of the largest protected areas in the east.

TN-01   TN-02

TN-03   TN-04

Design finalists for the Great Smoky
Mountains National Park quarter. The
Commission of Fine Arts recommended
alternative TN-03.

Shenandoah

Date: 2014
State: Virginia
Issue: 22 of 56
Mintmarks: P, D & S

A juvenile black bear at Old Rag Mountain in Shenandoah National Park, Virginia. *Photo by Daniel Lenski*

About the Featured National Park

Shenandoah National Park, at 130 square miles, is about twice the size of its nearby major city, Washington, D.C. Authorized by Congress in 1926, Shenandoah finally became a national park in 1935.

In the interim, President Herbert Hoover and his wife bought a parcel of land within the park to build their summer home, Rapidan Camp. They wanted to have a place to stay within a day's drive from Washington during the hot, humid summers. Hoover later donated Rapidan Camp's 13 buildings to the Commonwealth of Virginia in 1932 with the understanding it would be used as a presidential retreat. The last president to use it was Jimmy Carter in the late 1970s.

Skyline Drive, the park's main highway, has more than 75 scenic overlooks. There are over 500 miles of trails from which to see Shenandoah's amazing waterfalls and wilderness.

VA-01

VA-02

VA-03

VA-04

VA-05

Design finalists for the Shenandoah National
Park quarter. The Commission of Fine Arts
recommended alternative VA-05.

Arches

Date: *2014*
State: *Utah*
Issue: *23 of 56*
Mintmarks: *P, D & S*

Delicate Arch in Arches National Park, Utah.
Photo by Cedric Gouyvenoux

About the Featured National Park

Arches National Park, named a national monument by President Herbert Hoover in 1929 and redesignated as a national park in 1971, protects more than 2,000 natural sandstone arches. Landscape Arch, the longest in the park, measures an incredible 306 feet from base to base. More than 40 arches have naturally collapsed since 1970.

Arches National Park was used as a filming location for the 1965 Biblical epic, *The Greatest Story Ever Told.*

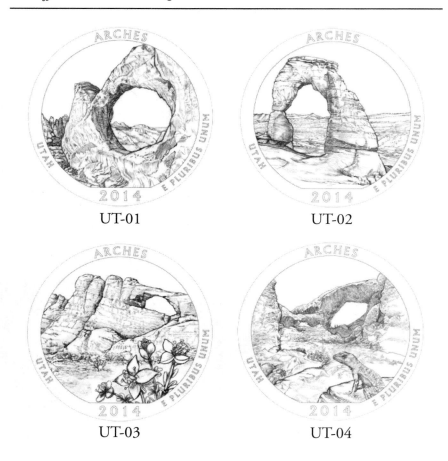

UT-01   UT-02

UT-03   UT-04

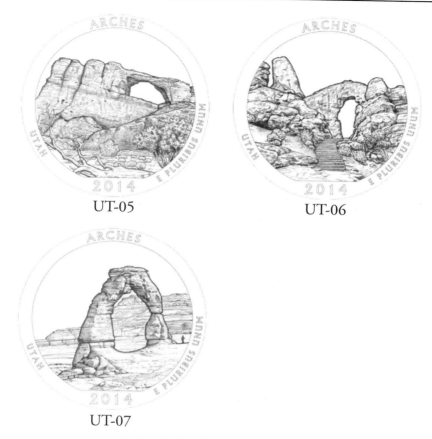

UT-05

UT-06

UT-07

Design finalists for the Arches National
Park quarter. The Commission of Fine Arts
recommended alternative UT-01.

Great Sand Dunes

Date: 2014
State: Colorado
Issue: 24 of 56
Mintmarks: P, D & S

Great Sand Dunes National Park, Colorado, with the Sangre de Cristo Mountains in the background. *Photo by Preiselbeere*

About the Featured National Park

Great Sand Dunes National Park and Preserve boasts the tallest dunes in North America, some rising upward of 750 feet off the floor of the San Luis Valley. A unique combination of weather and landscape is why the dunes continue to grow rather than erode. Visitors are free to climb, roll down, and even sled or ski down the enormous mounds of fine sand.

Explorer Zebulon Pike (namesake of Pike's Peak) wrote of Great Sand Dunes in 1807: "After marching some miles we discovered... sand-hills that extended up and down the foot of the White Mountains (today's Sangre de Cristos) about 15 miles and appeared to be about 5 miles in width. Their appearance was exactly that of a sea in a storm, except as to color, not the least sign of vegetation existing thereon."

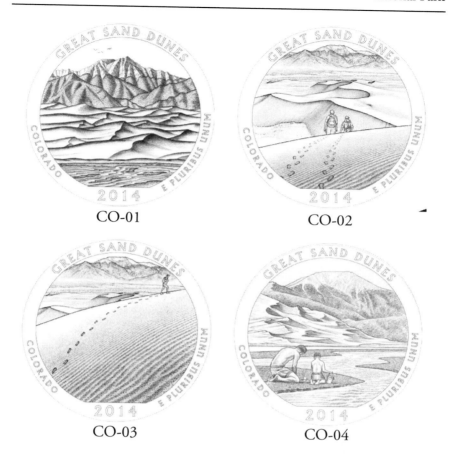

CO-01

CO-02

CO-03

CO-04

CO-05   CO-06

CO-07

Design finalists for the Great Sand Dunes
National Park quarter. The Commission of
Fine Arts recommended alternative CO-06.

Everglades

Date: 2014
State: Florida
Issue: 25 of 56
Mintmarks: P, D & S

A Barred Owl in Everglades National Park, Florida. *Photo by Chris Harshaw*

About the Featured National Park

The Everglades is a shallow basin in southern Florida with virtually its own unique ecosystem. It provides Miami with upwards of 20 percent of the city's fresh water supply.

Everglades National Park, though the third largest in the continental U.S. at 1.5 million acres, is only a small fraction of the entire Everglades.

The park protects some 800 species of diverse wildlife, from the Florida panther to the West Indian manatee. Due to man's close encroachment and damage from natural phenomenon, such as hurricanes, heat and more ordinary weather, it is currently on the Endangered World Heritage list.

FL-01   FL-02

FL-03   FL-04

FL-05   FL-06

Design finalists for the Everglades National
Park quarter. The Commission of Fine Arts
recommended alternative FL-04.

Homestead

Date: 2015
State: Nebraska
Issue: 26 of 56
Mintmarks: P, D & S

Grave of Daniel Freeman, who was believed to be the first
person to file a claim under the Homestead Act of 1862, in
Homestead National Monument of America, Nebraska.
Photo by Bill Dorr

About the Featured National Park

On July 4, 1861, President Abraham Lincoln declared that the purpose of our government is "to elevate the condition of men, to lift artificial burdens from all shoulders and to give everyone an unfettered start and a fair chance in the race of life." The Homestead Act of 1862 granted 160 acres of free land to claimants. Homestead National Monument of America, located in southeast Nebraska, commemorates this Act and the far-reaching effects it had upon the landscape and the people.

Visit Homestead National Monument of America to explore this tallgrass prairie landscape, tour historic buildings and view museum exhibits that tell the story of this important era of American history.

Kisatchie

Date: 2015
State: Louisiana
Issue: 27 of 56
Mintmarks: P, D & S

Longleaf Pine in Kisatchie National Forest, Louisiana. *Photo by Chris M*

About the Featured National Park

Kisatchie National Forest, located deep into the bayous, is full of majestic cypress groves and pine trees. Louisiana's only national forest offers an assortment of recreation activities including camping, picnicking, swimming, fishing, boating, hiking, hunting, horseback riding, off-road vehicles, sightseeing and bicycle riding. Two national recreation trails are located in the forest, the Wild Azalea Trail and the Sugar Cane Trail. Saline Bayou, which now features a 13-mile water trail, was designated a national scenic tributary in 1986.

Blue Ridge Parkway

Date: 2015
State: North Carolina
Issue: 28 of 56
Mintmarks: P, D & S

The Little Switzerland Tunnel on the Blue Ridge Parkway, North Carolina. *Photo by J.D. Shepard*

About the Featured National Park

As "America's Favorite Drive," the Blue Ridge Parkway National Park was designed as a slow-paced and relaxing drive, the ideal way to experience the natural and cultural history of the Appalachian Mountains. Almost 500 miles long, the north-south road meanders between the east and west facing slopes and varies in elevation from just under 650 feet at James River in Virginia to more than 6,000 feet south of Mt. Pisgah in North Carolina. Anyone who takes this drive around mid-to-late October will be rewarded with the leaves in full color.

Bombay Hook

Date: 2015
State: Delaware
Issue: 29 of 56
Mintmarks: P, D & S

Thousands of migrating ducks and geese at Bombay Hook National Wildlife Refuge, Delaware. *Photo by Jamie Richie*

About the Featured National Park

Bombay Hook National Wildlife Refuge in Delaware Bay covers 16,000 acres of tidal salt marsh, tidal pools and streams—a precious sanctuary and breeding ground for waterfowl in the fall, migrating shorebirds in the spring, and tall wading birds in the summer. Large numbers of horsecrabs and the eggs they lay in springtime is one reason over 250 species of birds have been spotted at Bombay Hook.

The Allee House, a pre-revolutionary war farmhouse on the National Register of Historic Places, is located on the refuge in near perfect condition.

Saratoga

Date: 2015
State: New York
Issue: 30 of 56
Mintmarks: P, D & S

Saratoga Tower at Saratoga
National Historical Park,
New York.

About the Featured National Park

The Battles of Saratoga, which took place separately on September 19 and October 7, 1777, was the first significant victory for the ragtag Continental Army during the Revolutionary War. In the initial clash, the sides fought to a stalemate, and the British retreated to wait for reinforcements which would never arrive.

General Benedict Arnold's reckless manuevers paid dividends, strengthing his growing reputation as a fearless patriot. Had he not later betrayed his countrymen, Arnold would have certainly been recognized as one of the great heroes of the war.

Saratoga National Historical Park contains a nine-mile road that visitors can drive, identifying American and British defensive positions, battle sites and monuments.

Shawnee

Date: 2016
State: Illinois
Issue: 31 of 56
Mintmarks: P, D & S

Garden of the Gods in Shawnee National Forest, Illinois.
Photo by Daniel Schwen

About the Featured National Park

Shawnee National Forest, tucked within the Ozark and Shawnee Mountains, is where massive rock formations and tree cover characterize the forest, which is markedly different from most of southern Illinois, where flat cornfields are predominant. Oak-hickory is the predominant timber, however, there are many other commercially important timber types. The 160-mile River-to-River Trail, which runs between the Ohio and Mississippi Rivers, is terrific for hiking, with certain areas available for equestrian use. Visitors also enjoy hunting, fishing, camping and other outdoor recreational activities.

Cumberland Gap

Date: 2016
State: Kentucky
Issue: 32 of 56
Mintmarks: P, D & S

Kentucky side of the Cumberland Gap Tunnel, which runs beneath Cumberland Gap National Historical Park and exits into Tennessee.
Photo courtesy Aaron Vowels

About the Featured National Park

Cumberland Gap, the most desirable place to cross the Appalacian Mountains for hundreds miles in either direction, was the first great gateway to the West. Three-hundred thousand pioneers traveled this route through the mountains into the wilderness of Kentucky in the late 18th century.

Cumberland Gap National Historical Park straddles Kentucky, Virginia and Tennessee. There are numerous trails and caves to explore in the park's 20,000 acres.

Harpers Ferry

Date: *2016*
State: *West Virginia*
Issue: *33 of 56*
Mintmarks: *P, D & S*

John Brown Fort at Harpers Ferry National Historical Park, West Virginia. *Photo by Joy Schoenberger*

About the Featured National Park

Harpers Ferry National Historical Park is a quaint, historic community at the confluence of the Potomac and Shenandoah Rivers. Stroll the picturesque streets full of 19th century landmark buildings, visit exhibits and museums, hike the trails and photograph famed Civil War battlefields.

Harpers Ferry changed hands between the Union and Confederate forces eight times. But the town is perhaps best known as the place where abolitionist John Brown attacked a Federal arsenal in 1859, two years before the war broke out. Brown's legacy led the Niagara Movement, the precursor to the National Association for the Advancement of Colored People, to hold their first meeting there.

Theodore Roosevelt

Date: 2016
State: North Dakota
Issue: 34 of 56
Mintmarks: P, D & S

A plains bison in Theodore Roosevelt National Park, North Dakota.
Photo by Matt Reinbold

About the Featured National Park

Theodore Roosevelt first came to North Dakota after the death of his wife, Alice Lee, who passed away during the childbirth of their daughter Alice. He said the badlands were "so fantastically broken in form and so bizarre in color as to seem hardly properly to belong to this earth." Roosevelt owned two ranches in North Dakota, the Maltese Cross Ranch and Elkhorn.

Theodore Roosevelt National Park is divided into three sections: the Southern Unit, the Northern Unit and Elk Ranch. Although the badlands is inhospitable to the extreme, the Southern Unit, which attracts most of the park's visitors, is home to bison, golden eagles, elk, prairie dogs, white-tail and mule deer, sharp-tailed grouse, wild horses, and pronghorns.

Fort Moultrie

Date: 2016
State: South Carolina
Issue: 35 of 56
Mintmarks: P, D & S

Fort Moultrie National Monument on Sullivan's Island, South Carolina. *Photo by D Dima*

About the Featured National Park

In 1776, nine British warships attacked the still unfinished fort on Sullivan's Island. Nine grueling hours later, Charleston was spared occupation, and the fort was named in honor of its commander, Colonel William Moultrie.

Over the next 35 years, the fort was razed twice, once from neglect and later from a hurricane. By 1860, Charleston had four forts ringing it main harbor. Just before the outbreak of the Civil War, Federal and Confederate forces took refuge on opposing sides. The Confederate Army soon bombed Fort Sumter, which began the bloodiest war in the history of the country.

Effigy Mounds

Date: 2017
State: Iowa
Issue: 36 of 56
Mintmarks: P, D & S

Sny Magill Unit at Effigy Mounds National Monument, Iowa.
Photo by Bill Whittaker

About the Featured National Park

An effigy mound is a raised pile of earth, often in the shape of an animal, religious symbol and other figures, constructed by Native American cultures perhaps as long as 2,500 years ago and believed to serve a religious function, such as a burial mound.

Effigy Mounds National Monument on the bluffs of the Mississippi River has 206 of these prehistoric mounds. From the ground, effigy mounds don't look like much, but an aerial view of the bear and bird shapes, some up to eight feet high and over 100 feet long, demonstrate why these artifacts are so fascinating.

Frederick Douglass

Date: 2017
Capital: District of Columbia
Issue: 37 of 56
Mintmarks: P, D & S

Frederick Douglass National Historic Site, District of Columbia.

About the Featured National Park

Frederick Douglass was born into slavery in a small rural community in Maryland. After two failed escape attempts, he used forged papers identifying him as a free black in the U.S. Navy. He boarded a train to New York City, and a day later found freedom. Douglass used his experiences in his writings and speaking engagements to highlight the horrors of the practice.

The Frederick Douglass National Historic Site remembers the most famous African American of the 19th century. His work to abolish slavery serves as a shining example of why the rights of all oppressed people are an important cornerstone of liberty and justice.

Ozark National Scenic Riverways

Date: 2017
State: Missouri
Issue: 38 of 56
Mintmarks: P, D & S

Alley Mill in Ozark National Scenic Riverways, Missouri.
Photo courtesy Christopher Friese

About the Featured National Park

Missouri's Ozark National Scenic Riverways is the first designated national park to protect a wild river system. More than 1.5 million visitors come to see the spring-fed rivers each year. Popular recreational activities include floating the rivers in canoes, kayaks or even inner tubes. Hunting and fishing are allowed in certain areas of the park. In addition, there are hundreds of caves to explore, some only accessible by boat. In the town of Alley, historic sites like the "Old Red Mill" and Welch Hospital are popular tourist attractions.

Ellis Island

Date: 2017
State: New Jersey
Issue: 39 of 56
Mintmarks: P, D & S

Immigration Museum at Ellis Island National Monument,
New Jersey. *Photo by Chensiyuan*

About the Featured National Park

Disturbing events in Europe, like the potato famine in Ireland and political unrest in Germany, led Europeans to the New World. Drawn to America by promises of things like the Homestead Act, they came by the millions.

When the federal government took over immigration from the states in the late 19th century, stations like Ellis Island were set up to keep undesirable immigrants from entering the country while people of means were usually able to bypass immigration stations More than 12 million "steerage-class" immigrants searching for the "American Dream" passed through Ellis Island between January 1892 and November 1954.

George Rogers Clark

Date: *2017*
State: *Indiana*
Issue: *40 of 56*
Mintmarks: *P, D & S*

George Rogers Clark National Historical Park in Vincennes, Indiana. *Photo by Mangus Manske*

About the Featured National Park

To capture the British garrison Fort Sackville in 1779, George Rogers Clark and his force of 170 Americans and Frenchmen made a miraculous, 18-day expedition, sometimes through freezing flood waters up to their shoulders. He was just 25 when he conceived of the audacious plan. Clark's leadership was the only thing that held them together.

The fort's capture gave the United States claims to the frontier, an area almost as large as the original 13 states. The inscription on Clark's statue at National Historical Park reads, "If a country is not worth protecting it is not worth claiming."

Pictured Rocks

Date: *2018*
State: *Michigan*
Issue: *41 of 56*
Mintmarks: *P, D & S*

Pictured Rocks National Lakeshore on Lake Superior, Michigan.
Photo by Chris

About the Featured National Park

Pictured Rocks National Lakeshore, the first national lakeshore, runs 42 miles along Lake Superior. The sandstone cliffs near Munising have been naturally formed into marvelously colorful arches and shallow caves.

The park also protects about 34,000 acres of Michigan's Upper Peninsula. Visitors come for the backcountry hiking and camping. Though Lake Superior's rough waters aren't friendly to small boats, the park is also home to three smaller, pristine lakes.

Apostle Islands

Date: 2018
State: Wisconsin
Issue: 42 of 56
Mintmarks: P, D & S

Hokenson Fishery, a part of the Little Sand Bay Visitor Center on the mainland of Apostle Islands National Lakeshore, Wisconsin. *Photo by Bobak Ha'Eri*

About the Featured National Park

On the northern tip of Wisconsin, Apostle Island National Lakeshore consists of 21 islands that are best viewed from the sea, which makes it a popular spot for experienced kayakers. Scuba divers can explore ancient shipwrecks and many underwater natural wonders. In winter, when Lake Superior freezes over, it's possible to explore the sea caves by foot.

Stockton Island boasts the largest concentration of black bears on the continent. Of the 50 miles of trails, the one from the visitor center on the mainland traverses a natural sand bridge to the main island in the park. Most of the islands have ranger stations, docks and camping.

Voyageurs

Date: 2018
State: Minnesota
Issue: 43 of 56
Mintmarks: P, D & S

Grassy Bay in Voyageurs National Park, Minnesota.
Photo by National Park Service

About the Featured National Park

Unlike most national parks, the primary access into Voyageurs National Park is by water. Although the park has 219,000 acres of land, it's mostly used as a destination for water enthusiasts. Houseboats, small motorboats, canoes and kayaks are very popular. In winter, recreational activities include snowmobiling, cross-country skiing, ice fishing and snowshoe hiking.

The park's name honors the French-Canadian fur traders and trappers who did business with the Ojibwe Indians in the Lake Rainy region about 200 years ago.

Cumberland Island

Date: 2018
State: Georgia
Issue: 44 of 56
Mintmarks: P, D & S

Wild stallion on Cumberland Island National Seashore, Georgia.
Photo by Bonnie Gruenberg

About the Featured National Park

The largest of Georgia's Golden Isles, Cumberland Island is a peaceful retreat, featuring long lazy beaches where visitors are able to collect seashells and look for other sea souvenirs. Hundreds of sea turtles come to the island each year to nest.

It's only 36,000 acres, so the Park Service restricts the number of visitors at Cumberland Island National Seashore to 300 at a time. The only way to reach the island is by boat, and you must make a reservation ahead of time.

Block Island

Date: 2018
State: Rhode Island
Issue: 45 of 56
Mintmarks: P, D & S

Bluffs of Block Island National Wildlife Refuge, Rhode Island. *Photo by Whitney*

About the Featured National Park

In the fall, Block Island National Wildlife Refuge is a resting point for more than 70 species of migratory songbirds. Young, inexperienced birds often miss the mainland and stop there before resuming their flights. In 1973, the refuge started from 28 acres of U.S. Coast Guard land, but donations and purchases have increased it to 129 acres.

Block Island is home to about permanent 1,000 residents. Birders and other wildlife enthusiasts are pretty much allowed to go wherever they want.

Lowell

The Great Gate, or "Francis' Folly," built in 1850, now part of Lowell National Historical Park, Massachusetts.

Date: 2019
State: Massachusetts
Issue: 46 of 56
Mintmarks: P, D & S

About the Featured National Park

Lowell National Historical Park encapsules the story of America's industrial revolution. It affords a look into the 19th century when the harnessed waterpower from the Merrimack River changed the textile industry in New England.

The park is comprised of many buildings of the era, including the world's largest textile museum. Inside there are nearly 100 exhibits designed to offer insight into the history of America's manufacturing industry.

American Memorial Park

Date: 2019
Territory: Northern Mariana
  Islands
Issue: 47 of 56
Mintmarks: P, D & S

American Memorial Park, commemorating the decisive battles of Siapan and Tinian during World War II, on the island of Saipan. *Photo by Abasaa*

About the Featured National Park

American Memorial Park honors the American and Marianas people who gave their lives during the Marianas Campaign of World War II. More than 5,000 names are inscribed on a memorial that was dedicated during the 50th anniversary of the Invasion of Saipan. Within the 133-acre boundary are beaches, sports fields, picnic sites, boat marinas, playgrounds, walkways and a 30-acre wetland and mangrove forest.

War in the Pacific

Date: 2019
Territory: Guam
Issue: 48 of 56
Mintmarks: P, D & S

War in the Pacific National Historical Park, Asan, Guam.

About the Featured National Park

War in the Pacific National Historical Park, located in Asan, Guam, commemorates the brave American, Japanese, Australian, Canadian, Chinese, French, British, New Zealander, Dutch and Soviet soldiers who fought and died in the Pacific Theater during World War II.

Visitors enjoy Guam's tropical climate and sandy beaches. Some 3,500 species of marine life, including 200 species of coral, are within the park's scuba and snorkeling areas.

San Antonio Missions

Date: 2019
State: Texas
Issue: 49 of 56
Mintmarks: P, D & S

Mission Concepción in San Antonio, Texas, part of the San Antonio Missions National Historical Park.

About the Featured National Park

Early in the 18th century, the proxy Spanish government in Mexico set up missions in Texas to acculturate and Christianize the native peoples and to ultimately make them Spanish citizens. In addition to being a part of the history of the Spanish colonial empire, the missions were a significant part of the history of Texas if not the entire Southwest region.

San Antonio Missions National Historical Park preserves four of the five missions built along the San Antonio River. (The most famous of them, the Alamo, is operated by the Daughters of the Republic of Texas.) Visitors are treated to an inside glimpse of what life was like for the Franciscan friars and mission Indians.

Frank Church River of No Return Wilderness

Date: 2019
State: Idaho
Issue: 50 of 56
Mintmarks: P, D & S

Middle Fork of the Salmon River in Frank Church River of No Return Wilderness, Idaho. *Photo by Rex Parker*

About the Featured National Park

At 2.3 million acres, Frank Church River of No Return Wilderness is the second largest protected area in the continental U.S. There are 2,600 miles of trails throughout the park's picturesque mountains and canyons. Camping, fishing, white water rafting and big game hunting name but a few of the recreational activities available.

The park was named in honor of Frank Church, the four-time democratic senator who sponsored the Wilderness Act in 1964, and four years later, the Wild and Scenic Rivers Act, which states rivers "shall be preserved in free-flowing condition, and that they and their immediate environments shall be protected for the benefit and enjoyment of present and future generations."

National Park

Date: 2020
Territory: American Samoa
Issue: 51 of 56
Mintmarks: P, D & S

Pola Islands just off the coast of Tutuila Island in National Park of American Samoa.

About the Featured National Park

National Park of American Samoa encourages visitors to explore the Islands of Sacred Earth, three volcanic and mountainous islands in the southwest Pacific Ocean. The only national park south of the equator, visitors can experience a tropical rainforest, lounge on radiant golden beaches and snorkel around dazzling coral reefs. Camping isn't allowed, but there are several hotels and even a program to stay with Samoan families.

Weir Farm

Studio of painter J. Alden Weir at Weir Farm National Historic Site, Connecticut. *Photo by Noroton*

Date: 2020
State: Connecticut
Issue: 52 of 56
Mintmarks: P, D & S

About the Featured National Park

Weir Farm National Historic Site commemorates the life of impressionist painter J. Alden Weir (1852—1919). The modest farmhouse became an enclave for painter friends, most notably Mahonri Young and Sperry Andrews. The landscape of the farm has been used in numerous works of art, including more than 250 by Weir himself, and continues to inspire a new generation of painters today.

Salt River Bay

Date: 2020
Territory: U.S. Virgin
* Islands*
Issue: 53 of 56
Mintmarks: P, D & S

Columbus expedition crew landing site at Salt River Bay National
Historical Park and Ecological Preserve, St. Croix, Virgin Islands.

About the Featured National Park

The United States purchased the Virgin Islands from Denmark in
1917, primarily to prevent the Germans from building a submarine
base there during World War I.

St. Croix is the only known site where a Columbus expedition set
foot in United States territory.

Salt River Bay National Historic Park and Ecological Preserve not
only commemorates the Columbus landing, but it also has one of the
largest mangrove forests in the Caribbean. Scuba divers and snorkelers
are rewarded with colorful coral reefs teeming with a variety of tropical
fish.

Marsh-Billings-Rockefeller

Date: 2020
State: Vermont
Issue: 54 of 56
Mintmarks: P, D & S

Home of George Perkins Marsh, widely regarded as the country's first conservationist and one namesake of Marsh-Billings-Rockefeller National Historical Park, Vermont.

About the Featured National Park

Marsh-Billings-Rockefeller National Historical Park captures a slice of all the beauty and charm Vermont has to offer—its covered bridges, stone walls, sugar maples and 400-year-old hemlocks.

Within the park is the oldest managed forest in the park system. Twenty miles of trails and carriage roads take visitors through one of the most compelling countrysides in the world. The park also houses a stunning art collection that includes paintings by landscape artists Albert Bierstadt, Thomas Cole and Edward Moran.

Tallgrass Prairie

Date: 2020
State: Kansas
Issue: 55 of 56
Mintmarks: P, D & S

Tallgrass Prairie National Preserve, Kansas.

About the Featured National Park

Of the 140-million acres of tallgrass praire that once blanketed the land between the Rocky Mountains and the Mississippi, only a small fraction remains. Tallgrass Prairie National Preserve seeks to protect 11,000 acres in the Flint Hills of Kansas.

Visitors can take self-guided tours of Rancher Stephen Jones' farm and walk the two-mile Southwide Nature Trail. Park management have plans to expand the prairie lands within the preserve and introduce bison herds.

Tuskegee Airmen

Date: *2021*
State: *Alabama*
Issue: *56 of 56*
Mintmarks: *P, D & S*

Hanger One Museum at Moton Field in Tuskegee Airmen National Historic Site, Alabama. *Photo by Rivers A. Langley*

About the Featured National Park

Before World War II, the U.S. military was reluctant to promote African Americans to officers. In the summer of 1941, an "experiment" to train an all-black fighter squadron proved they could fight in aerial combat every bit as well as whites. The "Red Tails," or "Red Tail Angels" to the bomber airmen they protected, were a highly decorated Fighter Group, earning the Distinguished Unit Citation.

Three years after the war, President Truman ordered the integration of the armed services, due in large part to the exemplary performance of the Tuskegee Airmen. Captain Benjamin Davis, one of 16,000 men and women who trained at Tuskegee, would go on to be the first African American general in the U.S. Air Force.

About the Author

DAVID L. GANZ, who turned 61 on July 28, 2012, is a multifaceted person. He has authored more than 30 books on topics from "A" (African literature) to "Z" (zoning law). A past president of the American Numismatic Association, he was appointed by President Nixon to the 1974 Annual Assay Commission.

In December 1993, U.S. Treasury Secretary Lloyd Bentsen appointed him a charter member of the Citizens Commemorative Coin Advisory Committee. He was reappointed in 1995 for a second one year term, leaving the office in February, 1996. His lasting accomplishment, which began with Congressional testimony in July, 1991 and onward, is the introduction of circulating commemorative coinage. This became a reality following his July, 1995 Congressional testimony in the form of the original 50 State Commemorative Coin Program— that began with Delaware in early 1999 and ended with the U.S. territories in 2009. In turn, the success of the State Quarters Program led to the National Park Quarters.

U.S. Mint Director Philip Diehl commented in 1998, "From my vantage point, the lion's share of the credit for making the 50 states program a reality goes to David Ganz for his persistence as an advocate..." It is worth highlighting that the U.S. government has made a substantial profit on these coins, returning over $5 billion to the American taxpayer.

A GRADUATE OF THE SCHOOL OF FOREIGN SERVICE at Georgetown University (Class of 1973), he took a law degree at St. John's University Law School and did post-graduate legal studies at New York University. He also studied international law at Temple University (Philadelphia) Law School in Rome, Italy, while working for the coins and medals office of the Food & Agriculture Organization of the United Nations. He consulted with FAO in Rome for more than 20 years, attached to both their legal office and their money and medals office.

In 1994, he was awarded the Order of St. Agatha (Commander) by the Republic of San Marino. In 2009, the Industry Council for Tangible Assets (ICTA) awarded him a "lifetime achievement" award.

Ganz has been asked to testify before the Subcommittee on Consumer Affairs and other subcommittees of the House Banking committee on more than a dozen occasions since 1974. He participated in the Senate Banking Committee's discussion on coin designs in September, 2001, and the House

Design proposal for the Arches National Park quarter. *Art rendering courtesy Danbury Mint*

hearing on "Coin & Currency Issues Facing Congress: Can We Still Afford Money" in 2006. He also submitted testimony before the Senate Banking Committee's field hearing on Foreclosure in 2009.

He is a county legislator who was re-elected in November, 2011 to his fourth term as a member of the Board of Chosen Freeholders of Bergen County, New Jersey. A freeholder since 2003, and now the longest serving Democratic freeholder in the 300-year history of the Board, Ganz served as the 29th Mayor of the Borough of Fair Lawn,

New Jersey, the fourth largest municipality in Bergen County for seven years, from 1999 to 2005. He was vice chairman of the freeholder board in 2005-6, chairman pro tempore in 2010 and has been chairman of the Budget Committee for eight consecutive years, from 2003 to 2010. As a freeholder, Ganz helps oversee Bergen County's annual budget of more than $600 million.

Committed to public service throughout his adult life, Ganz served on the Fair Lawn Zoning Board for 10 years before seeking election to the Borough Council in November, 1997. He was re-elected in 2001, leaving office as Mayor in January, 2006.

Design proposal for the Pictured Rocks National Park quarter. *Art rendering courtesy Danbury Mint*

A lawyer by profession, and the managing partner and principal litigator in the law firm of Ganz, Hollinger & Towe in New York City, and Ganz & Sivin, L.L.P. of Fair Lawn, N.J., Ganz has substantive service as a Committee Member of the State Legislation Committee of the Association of the Bar of the City of New York, as a member of the Civil Practice Law & Rules Committee of the New York State Bar Association (where he chaired the subcommittee on evidence and discovery), and the Civil Court Committee of the Queens County Bar Association.

He has served as a volunteer Small Claims Court arbitrator for more than 10 years in Queens County Civil Court, a contract mediator in the Bergen County Superior Court, and an arbitrator for the U.S. District Courts of the Eastern District of New York and the District of New Jersey. Ganz is one of only 71 statewide mediators certified by the U.S. District Court for entire state of New Jersey. He was sworn in as a Court Examiner by the New York State Appellate Division for the 2nd Judicial Department in December, 2011.

He also previously held positions as Rent Leveling Board Attorney in the City of Hoboken, N.J. and as Zoning Board Attorney in Paramus,

N.J. He is recognized in "Who's Who" in American Law and "Who's Who" in the United States. He served as Special Conflicts Counsel in Hoboken in 2005.

GANZ HAS BEEN AN AWARD-WINNING WRITER in the numismatic field for more than 45 years. His knowledge about coins and the law is widely sought after, both as a consultant, a writer and a lawyer. He served as a columnist for *Coin World* from 1976 to 1996 and for *Numismatic News Weekly* from 1969 to present. He wrote "Coin Market Insider's Report" each month for *COINage Magazine* from 1974 to 2009.

A prolific author in a variety of different fields, he has written more than 30 books, including a Random House mass-market paperback, *The Official Guide to America's State Quarters* (November, 2000), with more than 30,000 copies in print. A second edition in 2008 was given the Numismatic Literary Guild's special commendation.

He recently published *The Smithsonian Guide to Coin Collecting* (HarperCollins, April, 2008), another NLG-award winner, which was republished in a prestigious leather edition by Easton Press in 2010. *Profitable Coin Collecting* (Krause, 2008) and *Rare Coin Investing* (Krause, 2010) are recent books. *The Essential Guide to Investing in Precious Metals* was published by Krause Publications in December, 2011.

Other books include *A Critical Guide to Anthologies of African Literature* (African Studies Association, 1973, 2nd revised edition 2010), *14 Bits: A Legal & Legislative History of 31 USC §§324d-* (Three Continents Press, 1976), *The World of Coins & Coin Collecting* (Scribner's, 1980; 2nd edition, 1985; Bonus Books, 3rd edition, 1998), *Planning Your Rare Coin Retirement* (Bonus Books, 1998), *Guide to Commemorative Coin Values* (Bonus Books, 1999); *The 90 Second Lawyer* (Wiley, 1996), *How to Get an Instant Mortgage* (Wiley, 1997), and a number of law review articles.

Ganz edited a book on America's Coinage Laws (1792-1894) for Bowers & Merena in 1991. Recipient of the Numismatic Literary Guild's highest honor, the Clement F. Bailey Award (1996), he is a past recipient of its best writer award for *COINage Magazine, Coins Magazine, Coin World*, and *Numismatic News*.

Widely respected by his peers, he is listed in the Martindale-

Hubbell legal directory with an AV rating (highest rating), and his accomplishments are listed in Who's Who of American Law, and other Who's Who publications, including the Millennium edition of Who's Who in America. He is AvVo rated 10.0/10.0 (superb).

In his spare time, Ganz is a coin collector. A life fellow (one of 200 voting members) of the American Numismatic Society, he was appointed by President Nixon to the 1974 Annual Assay Commission, the oldest continually functioning committee in the federal government (dating to the founding of the Mint in 1792). He served from 1985 to 1995 as an elected member of the Board of Governors of the American Numismatic Association, the largest, educational non-profit organization of collectors in the world. He became the organization's 48th president in July, 1993, serving until August, 1995.

Design proposal for the San Antonio Missions National Park quarter.
Art rendering courtesy Danbury Mint

Ganz chaired the World Mint Council in 1994 and 1995 at its meetings held in conjunction with the American Numismatic Association annual convention. In 1995, more than 24 nations ministers attended Council meetings in Anaheim. He spoke at its plenary session, addressing delegates in Spanish, French, German, Russian and English. He is fluent in Spanish.

He has served as a consultant to the Canadian Olympic Coin Program (1973-76), the Moscow Olympic Coin Program (1976-80), for Occidental Petroleum and Lazard Freres in their 1981-2 Olympic Coin Program effort, the 1985-6 Statute of Liberty Centennial Celebration, and many others. His legislative expertise has been tapped by Olin Brass, Memorial Mission Hospital (for the Billy & Ruth Graham Congressional Gold Medal), the Platinum Guild, the Dutch Mint, the Portuguese State Mint, and others, on coin and related matters over the course of the past 20 years.

The World of Coins and Coin Collecting, of which *The Midwest Book Review* said the book "continues to be the complete guide for contemporary numismatics that knowledgeable collectors and professional investors refer to," is a bibliographic entry for the Encarta CD-ROM encyclopedia, Grollier's and many others. He also maintains the website www.AmericasStateQuarters.com to promote his book and the coin hobby.

As a lawyer, he has served as general counsel to the Professional Numismatists Guild, Inc. (1981-1993) and special counsel to the American Numismatic Association and the Industry Council for Tangible Assets, as well as ANA legislative counsel (1981-1996).

He and his wife, the former Kathleen A. Gotsch, are parents of three adult children and four felines. They have travelled to all seven continents.

Acknowledgements

I HAVE HAD A LOVE AFFAIR and an active role in national numismatic issues for more than 40 years. While in Washington attending the School of Foreign Service at Georgetown University in 1973, I was also the Washington correspondent for *Numismatic News Weekly*. I have seen sausages and laws made; neither is a pretty sight, but the end result can be worthwhile.

As a Washington correspondent, I met frequently with and attended hearings held by the chairmen of various committees with jurisdiction over numismatic matters, notably in the years Rep. Wright Patman, D-TX, chair of the Banking & Currency Committee, and his successor Rep. Henry Reuss, D-WI, Rep. Leonor K. Sullivan, D-MO, chairman of the subcommittee on Consumer Affairs (who handled coinage matters) and her successors on the re-named Subcommittee on Historic Preservation & Coinage, Rep. Robert Stephens, D-GA, and Del. Walter E. Faunteroy, D-DC.

From that involvement as a reporter, came a different role as an occasional consultant to the coinage subcommittee; that also entailed advocating particular positions—sometimes with the Mint favoring it, sometimes less so. In July 1995, when Congressman Castle held hearings on commemorative coinage, the State Quarters Program emerged, and it was clear the ways of the past were changing. Who would imagine after the difficult birthing process of the State Quarters Program that "America the Beautiful" would work so well coming up behind it?

No author, even when writing about something contemporaneous largely using original documents, acts alone; we all stand on the shoulders of those who preceded us. Thus, in looking at the selected bibliography, there are some old saws and chestnuts that find themselves repeatedly being used for the most unlikely of reasons. Books like *The Red Book* are not typically used for heavy research, but it is helpful to have collected in one place the size, weight and other statistical evidence of what coins are composed of in one place.

My thanks to Zyrus Press, and in particular to Bart Crane and Bruce Porter, for their longtime faith in the project, and their unique marketing into the non-numismatic community; Jennifer Casey, my editor on this project, is also acknowledged together with her two felines Rocky and Rambo.

Rep. Mike Castle and Rep. Carolyn Maloney present the reverse of the presidential one dollar.

My longtime friend Arthur Friedberg (whom I have known since he graduated from George Washington University, while I was studying at Georgetown University) for his astute comments and analysis in the front part of this book; my dear friend Reed Hawn, a famous collector who has been active in trying to obtain funding for the national parks and graciously agreed to write a brief forward to this book—it was his persistence in nudging me about a number of pending bills that ultimately made me decide to talk to Zyrus about adding this book to their roster. Thanks to Kevin Flynn for sharing with me his one-man research enterprise, but mostly for recommending Zyrus as a publisher.

Special thanks to former mint director Philip Diehl, now in private industry marketing and merchandising precious metal products, for his gracious introduction, and for the deep friendship that developed when we both served with Reed Hawn on the Citizens Commemorative Coin Advisory Committee a generation ago. Philip has been very public in giving me credit for the circulating State Quarters Program, which is the progenitor of the national park issue, but in fact once he was persuaded the idea had merit, he became an important and strong backer who made the difference between the program first coming on board, then between success and failure. He may not take credit for it publicly, but there are those of us who know how many good ideas fail for lack of critical backing—and he provided it.

I am grateful for the professionalism and record keeping of the Commission of Fine Arts, and in particular Sue Kohler with whom I worked closely when I was a member of the Citizens Commemorative Coin Advisory Committee, and then afterwards, even as she moved into retirement and part-time consulting. She and Charles Atherton, a CCCAC member whose untimely death robbed the Fine Arts Commission, the Mint, the CCCAC and its successors of a brilliant analyst and memorialist, who made sure that recommendations and changes were made for the right reasons.

More recently, the Commission of Fine Arts and its staff, including Susan Ramosa, technical information specialist for the Commission of Fine Arts, were of significant help. So, too, was Michael White, of the U.S. Mint, and the staff and members of the Citizens Coinage Advisory Committee. Thanks to Arnetta Caine, a friend of many years for helping with the navigation of people supporting the Mint's website.

Design proposal for the Ellis Island National Park quarter. *Art rendering courtesy Danbury Mint*

My friend Donald Scarinci, a well known lawyer in Northern New Jersey, was an invaluable member of the CCAC. We met many years ago through the course of our day jobs. One day he asked if I was somehow related to the guy who he'd read occasionally in coin periodicals; since he had read that author for many years, he wondered if the similarity in name might lead to a happy coincidence. We have been close friends ever since. Donald and I always try and find time to talk about more than local politics. We talk about coin collecting like other guys talk about sports. Many thanks to him for making his files and papers available and discussing the National Parks Program with me. Also to Helene Rotondo, of Scarinci & Hollenkack in Lyndhurst, N.J., for acting as our middleman and follow-through.

Two individuals who have helped in the same way from different offices are Robert Pantina, who served as my freeholder aide for about three years, on the campaign trail for two re-election campaigns on the freeholder board, and has now moved on to work for the Bergen County Clerk, my friend John Hogan, and Hannah Seo, an administrative and executive assistant in my New York law office, Ganz & Hollinger, P.C. I appreciate the effort that each of them made in helping me stay on deadlines, and occasionally helping me secure data needed to complete this book. My law partners of 30 years, Jeri Hollinger and Teri Towe, still wonder when this writing thing might slow down a bit, but they remain supportive of me and my quirky style.

Kathy Ganz, my wife and biggest supporter, sometimes feels that books are my life. Actually, she is, but the books are a way for me to relax and also leave a legacy that will be available for as long as there are books and research libraries. I thank her profusely for allowing me to pursue my passions and for being so understanding and supportive.

Mimi, one of four felines in our home, deserves an honorable mention. She knows when to purr sweetly in my home office, telling me it's time to pack it in for the night. Mimi and her furry sisters have taken the roles of my three grown children who are now busy with their own lives. Only one of them casually collects coins, but all are familiar with the State Quarters and National Park Programs, which they have found addictive.

Lastly, thanks for reading my "Under the Glass" column that has run in *Numismatic News* since 1969 and for continuing to read the books that follow. As far as I'm concerned, this hobby of numismatics has become more than an investment and hobby—it's a lifestyle that I expect will figure prominently in my retirement plans.

David L. Ganz
Fair Lawn, New Jersey
April 17, 2012

State and National Park Index

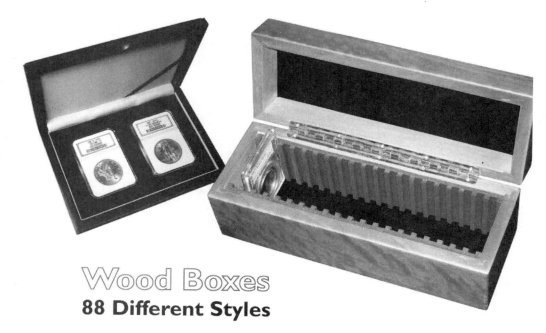